https://www.jerriebarber.com

Fleecy Clouds

This memoir is a truthful recollection of actual events in the author's life. Some conversations have been recreated and/or supplemented. The names and details of some individuals have been changed to respect their privacy.

ISBN: 979-8-218-03165-7
Paperback Edition

Cover and interior design: Joey Sparks

https://www.jerriebarber.com

Fleecy Clouds

One Woman's Story of Surviving and Thriving after Childhood Abuse

From the Heart of a Champion

Gail Champion Barber

and Alice Sullivan

Wedding Picture

Anniversary Picture

Dedicated to
Jerrie Barber

My husband for 58 years,
who encouraged me to put
my story in book form.

My favorite

Preacher

Ventriloquist

Barefoot Runner

Praise for *Fleecy Clouds*

"Thank you, Gail Barber, for sharing your life story. It was heartbreaking, yet heartwarming. This book is not just for women who have been abused; there are many faces of abuse that show no respect of gender. We male survivors see ourselves in the cracked mirror you hold up. Your therapist James Jones did us all a great favor when, years ago you were inclined to 'never talk about this again,' he offered this counsel: 'Gail, it would be a shame to waste all that pain.' Many readers will be glad you listened."
—Eddie J. Miller

"Much of my reading of your story has been through tears. Now, this is a marvel because I do not cry very easily at all, for any reason. The reason for this is one of my own secrets.

Wonderfully written through the eyes, ears, and heart of a child. Your book will do much good. Like the ripples created by your rocks thrown into the water, it will radiate outward from soul to soul. Who best to appreciate the grace and love of God and Christ, than the soul that has abode long in Lo Debar? (2 Samuel 9).

Most definitely, those who read Gail's book will be blessed. At age seventy-five, and with hindsight, we garner a heap of knowledge that can benefit others. I am thankful Gail found help and is now willing to help others. Fortunate indeed is the person who has no secrets."
—Charlene Rigney

"Thank you, Mrs. Gail, for sharing your story with me. I'm excited to think of how helpful and hopeful your experiences will be for others, especially women who have hardships and circumstances in their lives that seem impossible to overcome."
—Jill Parham

"Thank you for giving me the opportunity to read the book of your life. Some chapters were heart-wrenching and I didn't know if I could continue to read! Those memories were probably just as difficult for you to write.

But your years at Childhaven helped to ease your pain and even surpass that into a positive, blessed experience. It has helped to make you into the amazing lady that you are today. I'm grateful to those who invested in you, and in the dividends that investment has paid."
—Laurel Sewell

"Ms. Gail came into my life when I needed her to, and I didn't even know it. Reading her story, knowing her, seeing where she came from and experienced makes me see God's hand very clearly in all our lives. Wonderful, wonderful book!"
—Sandy Turnbow

"Gail, my sweet friend, I have devoured your book, every word. It has me wrapped up and has touched me on so many levels. Blessings to you as you write and relive so many horrible memories. Even knowing the 'end' and being your friend for so many years, it has touched me deeply."
—Cheryl Pitts

"Gail, thank you for sharing your story. When you and Jerrie were sitting behind me in chapel at FHC, I saw joy and would never have dreamed you went through this trauma. This heartbreaking story needs to be shared, because it speaks of resilience, of joy in spite of pain."
—Deanna Brooks

"I enjoyed the book. It was easy to read. It was, and is, wonderful. It broke my heart to learn about the horrible life Gail lived after losing her mom and being in Mammy's house. I thank God for Childhaven and what it meant to the many children who were able to call it home."
—Wayne Kilpatrick

"Thank you so very much for sharing your remarkable story! I have always loved and admired you for who you are but now so much more knowing where you have been. Your story was written in such an intriguing way I couldn't put it down. Thank you for 'putting yourself out there' and showing us how even the worst burdens can be turned into blessings. I know this book will be such a blessing to many who have struggled to overcome their own adversities and become 'champions' over their own trials."
—Sandra Parker

"Gail, I have always just loved you like my own mother, and now even more I realize why! I can't tell you the last actual book I read from cover to cover . . . unrelated to the Bible. If I had time, tireless eyesight, and no distractions, I wouldn't have been able to put your book down! I'm so excited for Gail and for all those her story will surely impact in positive ways."
—Ronnie Kephart

"This book is a Champion! It is a treasure. You'll devour it! I read each chapter cheering for little Gail. I've known Sister Barber for years, but I was not prepared for a book this gut-wrenching, this compelling, this masterfully crafted. You'll want to support and encourage every young child you meet after you read this book.

Thank you, Gail, for sharing your life with others!"
—Dale Jenkins

I started reading this around 7 o'clock tonight and just couldn't find a place to stop. I have just now finished and had to tell you that I have been deeply moved by your story. I have also been tremendously blessed. You have driven home a lesson that I needed to relearn. That is to try to be more aware of the pain others have experienced. Thank you for this blessing.
—Ron Harper

"It is a remarkable story of Gail's tenacity and God's protective hand that has led her to give us this written treasure of her life. I think everyone who has experienced trauma or knows someone who has had trauma in their life can benefit from reading *Fleecy Clouds*.
—Gwen Zimmerly

Table of Contents

"I've never read the story of a great man without finding that at one time or another in that man's life he went through days of hurt, and it was the molding influence of the hurt that made the man what he was. It's a great principle for life, it's the heart of a champion."

—Bob Richards, *The Heart of a Champion, Inspiring True Stories of Challenge and Triumph*

Foreword

Secrets Need Not Define Us

"And we know that in all things God works
for the good of those who love him,
who have been called according to his purpose."
—Romans 8:28

Most of us hold secrets. Secrets that we rarely share with others, even our spouses or our best friends. They may be too painful to share—the result of physical abuse, molestation, or some other form of trauma. We may feel ashamed, even if we are the victim. Our secrets can be like a heavy weight that we just carry around each day, affecting our lives while we seek to present a smiling face to the world. When asked how we are doing, we are always "doing fine" even when we are not. Until the weight becomes so heavy that we just begin to shut down . . . Thoreau describes this existence as "lives of quiet desperation." We just want to break free, to break out from the darkness!

For over twenty-seven years I was privileged to serve as Executive Director at Childhaven, Inc. a Christian children's home. Childhaven serves foster youth, all of whom have experienced child abuse, ranging from molestation, violence, or some other form of neglect, such as starvation. Many have grown up in poverty and most are well acquainted with our land's growing addiction problem (drugs, alcohol, sex.) Nearly all have learned to hold their secrets tightly within themselves. It affects lives—evidenced by their sleep and eating disorders, anger issues, and depression, to name just a few.

But many, if not most, of these young people can find a way to deal with their pasts in a healthy manner. In fact, many will thrive in adulthood. To do so they must find a place of safety, acceptance, and understanding. A place where faith in a caring, loving, and gracious God can be planted, nurtured, and developed. This is Childhaven's goal—to be just such a place!

I remember visiting with a young lady in the hallway of Childhaven's offices. She often came through greeting the staff after getting home from school. On this day she said to me, "Do you know what has happened to me?" I acknowledged that I did not. Her entire demeanor changed, becoming so very dark and cloudy and she said, "I just can't talk about it. It's why I can't sleep at night unless the lights are all on." Then she slowly walked away. She was like so many children at Childhaven with dark, secret, painful pasts, often unable to talk about them.

I met Gail Champion Barber decades ago. Her husband Jerrie serves on the board of directors at Childhaven, and they truly love Childhaven! We had often visited during reunions, Holiday events, in our offices, and over dinner. Gail is an amazing woman. Little did I know just how amazing.

Some time back, they shared with me their plans to write this book. I encouraged Gail to proceed. At the very least, it would be such a special volume for her family. They would cherish it for generations to come. Time passed by, then a manuscript came.

I learned that though I thought I knew my good friend Gail, I really had no idea about all that she had experienced and overcome. In this book, you see into the heart and soul of its author. The pain, ritual abuse, poverty, and the power of family are so openly discussed. You are invited into the depths of her mind and heart. You will experience her pain. But you will also see her great faith, true grit, determination, and unconquerable spirit. The story shared is not only one of survival but one of thriving. Gail is not just writing about how to survive an abusive childhood—she has lived it and survived. Not just survived, as she always has a smile on her face, an encouraging word to share, and is fully enjoying life!

Gail Champion Barber has spent her life helping others. She often speaks at conferences and to women's groups. She shares her story. She takes a genuine interest in others and has changed countless lives. Her love for the Childhaven Children's Home is obvious. And in this volume, she shares stories of others of the Childhaven family in a powerful and endearing way.

This book was written to help you. You will be encouraged to deal with those secret demons that may be a part of your life. (We all have them, you know.) Your faith will be encouraged, and you will be challenged to live your life for others. In short, your life will be changed in a positive and encouraging way.

You may also fall in love with Childhaven, a place that has touched countless lives over the decades. To learn more about the ministry of Childhaven, visit www.childhaven.com.

Thank you, Gail. Your willingness to let us see deeply into your soul will not only enrich our lives but the lives of all who will read this book in the years to come!

Dr. Jim Wright
Executive Director Emeritus
Childhaven, Inc.
2022

Introduction

May You Find a Blessing in This Book

I have a great God-blessed life, and I'm thankful. I grew up at Childhaven Children's Home in Cullman, Alabama. The four years before going there were difficult. My mother died when I was five years old. Several foster homes, times when I was separated from my brothers and sister, and physical abuse from a relative took a toll on me.

A few years after marrying and having two children, the nightmares and association of previous pain became difficult to deal with. Thankfully, James Jones, a counselor and marriage and family therapist, began to work in our building at the Central Church of Christ in Dalton, Georgia, in January 1982. I started seeing him, learning how to deal with my pain. He was tremendously helpful. We worked more on how and when to share my story with others.

I've learned there are times when someone needs professional help to deal with trauma. That is nothing to be ashamed of.

Jerrie and I have now worked with thirteen congregations since my therapy with James. I tell my story to a ladies' Bible class or other groups soon after arriving. I've spoken to many ladies' days where I've shared my story. These events provided opportunities for others to share their stories and get help for the first time.

Last fall, I started working with a professional writer, Alice Sullivan, to share my story. I have written much through the years in longhand. Alice is helping me arrange this so it will be interesting and helpful.

I hope you find a blessing in this book that will add to your life and you can share with others.

A difficult beginning didn't ruin the remainder of my life.

And it doesn't need to ruin yours, either.

Chapter 1

The Haunted Girl in the White Slip

"You can't go back and change the beginning, but you can start where you are and change the ending."
—C.S. Lewis

The night before I saw therapist James Jones, I awoke drenched in sweat, unable to breathe. Desperate for relief, I clutched my chest, wincing through the physical sensations that were rooted in something psychological. Hot shame spread through my temples to my cheeks and jaws. Almost identical to the sensation of nausea, it tingled and caught in my throat. I knew releasing it would not be as easy as hovering over a porcelain toilet with my hair pulled back.

After a few minutes of mental anguish, I laid back and focused my eyes on the popcorn ceiling. I inhaled, attempting to recover any memory from a dream I might have had. What had been so triggering to wake me up in such a panic? Though moments prior I had been sleeping, there were no lasting images of where I had drifted off to, nor recollection of whom I'd been speaking with. There was only the radiating, emotional pain that I'd been trying to avoid since childhood. Instead of fading with each infrequent fuzzy memory, the pain only seemed to worsen as the years passed.

Sometimes while experiencing these nightmares, I would hurt myself by accidentally hitting my head on the bed post, falling off the bed, or kicking and flinging my arms and legs so hard I would pull a muscle or worse. One incident required surgery to recover. Often after these terrible dreams, I would have marks on my back like scratches that were deep enough to scab.

Now at forty-three years old, the anxiety and fear had become so consuming—even causing a few fainting spells—that I agreed to seek help. It was affecting both my daily life and my family. I did not want to pass on my traumatic past to my children.

The anguish surfaced in strange ways, particularly around old women. Not always, but most of the time. I had managed to hide my anxiety as much as I could around others. But anytime I saw a woman with gray hair, especially if she was walking in my direction or made eye contact, I went into survival mode. I always tried to walk away, to avoid any kind of conversation, or worse—physical touch in the form of a hug, a handshake, a kiss on my cheek, or a tap on my shoulder or forearm. While their gray hair caused an immediate worry, the women's hands were truly my enemy, especially if they were damaged by arthritis.

My husband Jerrie knew to keep a protective eye on me at church. Those holy spaces should have felt incredibly safe and peaceful, but they were where I was the most vulnerable. I was all too easily cornered in busy foyers by grandparents (with grandchildren in tow), who often asked to take us out to lunch. Any time Jerrie stepped away I felt exposed, so we developed a secret alerting system. Anytime I needed an escape, I would slip out of my location or conversation casually to find Jerrie and give him a nod. That was his sign to come to my aid and provide a distraction so I could remove myself from the situation. These situations were occurring more and more frequently.

While most older women terrified me, there were a few precious women who did not. Mrs. Mitchell was someone I could trust. She never frightened me. Perhaps it is because the first time I met her she gave me a fancy handbag with ten dollars tucked away in the pocket. Instantly I felt that this woman was kind and not a threat. I was even comfortable embracing her. She had class, and her husband complemented her perfectly—still opening the passenger door for her, always being gentle and intentional with his delicate cargo. She'd wave at everyone like royalty as she left the church parking lot. Even at people she hardly knew. But she always meant it.

Mrs. McCoy was another woman I had come to enjoy. She was a Southern, soft-spoken, gentle lady. She dressed beautifully. She kept a locket around her neck with photos of her grandchildren inside. But the first time her lips met my cheek, it was too much. I suffered momentarily, and even more so when I noticed her hands. They opened as she embraced me and I cringed, thinking for a brief moment that she might slap me. Her hands—withered by time, damaged by arthritis—looked like Mammy's. Then in a half-second, she *was* Mammy, and I was frozen.

Too easily, *all* of these women were Mammy, my grandmother.

My body always hurt when they'd embrace me. I'd remember Mammy's disdain and her willingness to strike without warning. No matter how gentle Mrs. McCoy's kisses were, they'd mimic the same external flush as though I had been slapped across my face. Pleasantries would happen in slow motion as my mind went blank, until Jerrie would ground me with his touch. Back to reality.

Retreating sometimes worked unless the women were aggressively friendly. Southern churchgoers tended to be excessively sweet—with their courteousness, casseroles, and Christmas cards that I'd always hang on the refrigerator. There were certainly some of these women that I almost hated—I just never wanted to be honest about it; it wasn't the upright thing.

On one occasion, one such aggressively nice lady rounded the corner of the main lobby, heading in my direction, while I was waiting for Jerrie. I would have crawled into the cracks between the crimson cushions on the chairs if they could have held me. In my younger years, I'd developed the ability to go to sleep at will as a means of escape. I'd position myself in *comfortable enough* places, then slip into a dream state. As the woman neared me, I considered suddenly dozing off—perhaps later blaming it on medication.

But she was too close—way too close. Way too fast. She neared my chair and I pulled back. After she was practically sitting in my lap, I stood and made my way past her to the staircase. The further I climbed, the more she chased, chatting all the way. I moved to the right side of the stairs, and she followed me. Then I stepped to the left and she did the same. I took a few uncomfortable backward steps up the stairs and she stepped up to close the distance between us.

By the end of our conversation, we'd made our way around the building before Jerrie located me. Once I was safely in the car with him, I felt like I'd gotten in a solid workout. When I told him what happened, he laughed about the marathon and asked me what the conversation with the woman was about. I'd been so busy running; I honestly couldn't remember. I wondered how something so minor could feel so exhausting—but many of these scenarios depleted me.

There was nothing more insufferable than being trapped in vulnerable moments with most of these women. What was meaningful for them was usually harmful for me. On one Wednesday night, a lady I usually avoided approached me to ask if I would like to hear a poem she had written. Instantly, I felt trapped.

"Of course!" I lied—recoiling internally as she leaned forward and put one arm around my neck. She then began to recite the poem by memory in my ear. Her tone was gentle, maternal, soothing even. Yet, after a few lines, I felt hot tears pooling in my eyes from feeling terrified, worried I might faint. I let them roll down my face and neck, wondering what I should say in response. Then anger surfaced, eclipsing my vulnerability. After that, I felt the familiar, hot shame in my cheeks.

Finally, she was done with her recitation, and she looked at my wet face, no doubt thinking I was crying because I had been so moved by the beauty of her poem. "I knew you would understand. It makes me cry, too!" she told me. And then she walked away.

That was one of the emotional experiences I told James Jones about when I sat in his office for the first time. As I ran my hands over the threads of the fabric in the sunken floral couch, my timid voice filled the whole room with sound. It was an unfamiliar feeling—to hear my own voice; to share my pain, my fears, and my innermost feelings with someone other than Jerrie. I was feeble and something was emerging in me, far too much to bear alone. I could no longer continue living life as I had since my abuse at ages six and seven at the hands of my grandmother, Mammy.

James listened patiently and didn't give any indication that he was critically judging me. My husband had known him for years. They had become friends over time, which gave me a level of comfort in speaking with him. James and his boys spent the night at our house now and then when he held church workshops in the area.

It felt safe to sit in his office. He never treated me like I was strange. I felt my secrets were safe in the safety deposit box of his mind. But it didn't feel safe yet to share my whole story. I whispered and skimmed over the hard parts that had never been spoken. There was a lot I didn't say. James affirmed that this was natural with trauma survivors; that healing would take time.

He said to establish trust with him, he'd start giving me weekly homework. Afterward, we'd debrief. After a few weeks, my first assignment was to tell my story to two people—specifically, two women. Two people were *a lot* of people. But he said that once I shared my story, others would likely begin to open up to me as well.

The first woman I talked to cried the whole time I spoke, feeling immense empathy for me. The second woman didn't seem to be paying attention at all. I wasn't sure which response hurt worse. After I finished confiding in my silent friend, she surprised me by asking if she could share her lifetime secret with me.

It was horrible, agonizing. She had seen a murder as a child. The murderer had seen her too and had threatened to kill her parents if she told. Not even her husband knew the secret she'd been holding onto for decades. We held each other and cried freely afterward. She felt relieved to have told her truth to at least one person, and I felt honored that she had confided in me.

What James had promised me was materializing: as I opened up to others, they opened up to me. I was grateful to relieve my friend of her burden. Now there were two people who knew her secret, and that was enough. I relayed this proudly in therapy. It was my first mark of progress.

Next, James made me go to the nursing home alone to visit two old women from the church. I prayed for courage as I imagined what their hands might look like. I was tempted to tell him *I wasn't ready,* but I pressed on.

They are sick, old people. I told myself. *They can't hurt me. They aren't Mammy.*

Because I wouldn't see James until the next Monday, I waited until Friday. I thought, *I'll just do it and get it over with—then process over the weekend.*

I had visited nursing homes often with church groups, but never alone. Even parking out front was difficult. With great fear, I entered one of the most unpleasant places a person can go. The smell of cafeteria food and sanitizer wafted through the rotating doors. I held my breath, trying not to make eye contact with the gaunt residents sleeping in wheelchairs throughout the entry hall. I clutched two small gifts tightly in my hands. I wondered if the women would like them.

I found room 107 with little effort, and knocked on the partially open door with dread, but peered in to find an empty, unmade bed. The woman was away. It was the perfect test run. One down, one to go.

My second visit felt a little easier, like a pressure valve was loosening, as I made my way past the warmly lit game room where music was playing. The residents were doing crafts. Every now and then I'd hear affirmations and clapping as a resident was praised for their good work. When I reached room 219, I found another resident chatting with the woman I'd come to see. The woman and I spoke for a little while, and the conversation transitioned from awkward stammers to full sentences relatively quickly. I was surprised—pleased even. I gave my two gifts to these women.

I walked out into the weekend having accomplished my goal. Then I slid into the warm leather seats of my car and cried. When I told James later, he cried too. I felt safe—almost safe enough to tell him about several experiences that I'd never spoken about to anyone—experiences that were still so poignant, potent, and clear in my mind.

Gail at five years old: "Little Me"

The first time it happened, I was in my mid-teens and living at Childhaven, a children's home in Cullman, Alabama. I was sitting on my bed, staring off into space, when suddenly, in front of me I saw an exact replica of myself as a child, standing in a beautiful white cotton slip. Little Me was crying, so I reached for myself, thinking my hands would run through my younger self like a ghost. But Little Me was a person, whole and real. This *wasn't* my imagination. So, I drew Little Me to myself. She had no weight. I sat her on my lap and tried to tell her everything would be all right. But I couldn't make the crying stop because Little Me didn't trust me. The truth was, I hoped everything would turn out all right, but I wasn't even sure myself.

I wondered if I should tell someone about what had happened. I had houseparents and other children to talk to, but this story seemed too unbelievable to share. The children at Childhaven didn't have counselors back then as they do now. We were each other's counselors. We all had stories, but mine seemed too unbelievable to share. I thought about it for days but never told anyone.

This happened a handful of other times over the next few years—once in college, again early in my marriage, then after I had children.

I began to see Little Me more often after a traumatic accident in 1977 when Jerrie and I were in a fire at church camp.

There was a little house where we taught crafts to the campers. I had told one boy in particular, "Do not come back in here by yourself." He and his sister were sent to camp by a church. They didn't know how to mind. They didn't know they were supposed to do what they were told to do. Their mother lived in a little trailer, and if the kids wanted to go to school, they went. And if they didn't want to go, they didn't have to go. When I gave him instruction, he didn't listen.

He had entered the craft house and turned on the burner where we had been making candles. The wax caught on fire. When we saw the fire, Jerrie and I rushed into the building to put it out. Jerrie grabbed the container of wax to get it outside. I threw a towel over it, which forced the flames higher. Jerrie slung the container to get it out of the building and the flaming hot wax landed on my legs and face.

Thankfully, the building didn't catch on fire. The place was soon full of children. I thought they were taught to go away when there was a fire, but instead they all ran in to see what happened. I sat on the floor and started wiping the wax off my legs and wiping it on the floor.

An hour later, I made it to what would later become the burn unit at Erlanger in Chattanooga. It was a very long recovery. My face, my right arm, and both of my legs were burned badly.

The following summer the little boy told me he was sorry.

While the visitations with Little Me occurred in different years, the visual was always the same: Little Me always wore a white cotton slip and was always crying.

Over time, and with my constant reassurance, Little Me cried less. Once we established a sense of safety and trust between us, we could read each other's minds. She'd open up to me about her feelings, and I'd tell her about her future, a future I hoped was brighter than any darkness we'd endured.

Maybe because of the trauma to my body from the burn accident, weeks in the hospital with months of recovery, I focused so much on healing I saw none of Little Me for a period of time. I missed my visits with myself, but I felt Little Me needed me less. Maybe I was healing after all.

James Jones and I saw each other for over one year. I made great progress. When we completed therapy because we moved to a new church, I said, "Thank you for your help but I don't ever want to talk about this again." James said, "Gail, it would be a shame to waste all that pain."

His reply blessed me and hundreds of other people.

Chapter 2

Little House

"Look at how good and pleasing it is when families live together as one."
—Psalm 133:1

Wayne was Mama's firstborn—a gorgeous, writhing bundle of expression, warmth, and love. Daddy's sentiment about his first son's birth never changed; he'd retell the story with glistening eyes—his smile marked by nostalgic pride. As Wayne laid on Mama's chest, learning her breath and heartbeat, Daddy admired his tiny form, swaddled in soft blue cloth. He was perfect in every way, except for a small open spot on his spine. (He was born with spina bifida, a congenital disability which effects the spine of a fetus.)

When the doctors first told my parents about the hole, the breath left their bodies. Mama's sensitivity made her panic, while Daddy's unbridled hope kept him optimistic.

The year was 1940, and treatment options were limited. *It won't be serious,* the doctor promised Daddy when they began conversations about surgery. Wayne was eighteen months old, and just beginning to walk well, when he was admitted to a Methodist hospital near Memphis, Tennessee. Daddy always liked to tell people that Wayne once walked.

As his surgeon explained the risks of the complex procedure, Mama cradled Wayne's head and held back tears. It would be an experimental surgery—the most innovative practice in the nation. Though general anesthesia would have been sufficient, it was decided that Wayne would be given an epidural with the largest needle my parents had ever seen.

Sadly, the shot paralyzed him below the waist. Wayne was given only two years to live. But his ferocious spirit and bright will to survive kept him transcending the odds. Wayne's hope eclipsed the limitations the external world put on him. He was a source of light whose vitality would ensure him a whole eighty years of exuberant thriving.

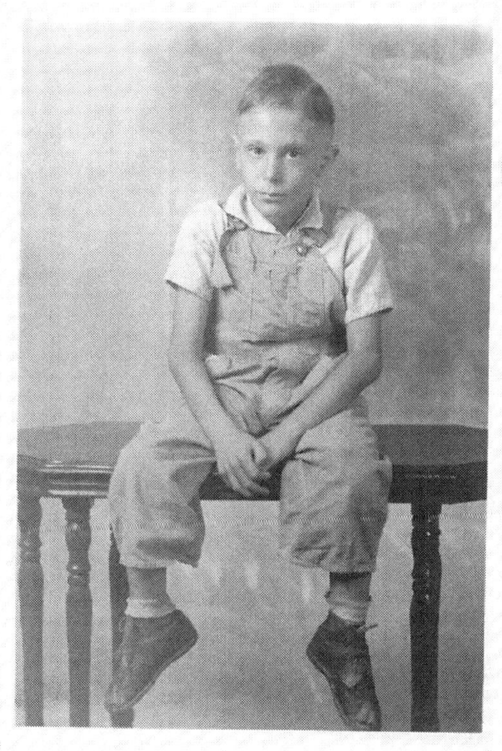

Wayne Champion at seven years old

As a little girl, I believed my oldest brother to be possibly wiser than Daddy, who was almost impossible to surpass in my eyes. Despite the complications of Wayne's wheelchair, and the pain of seeing my parents care for him while we lived in poverty, Wayne's story was one of determination and grace. We were lucky to have it woven into the fabric of our family. It was as if the best pieces of Daddy and Mama had mixed for a holier lesson than any of us could have imagined. Even the days of suffering were profound, with Wayne there to make sense of them. He was the greatest teacher of the family, and certainly hard to live up to. Wayne's personality never detracted from the sweetness of my younger brother Don.

Though I was far too little to absorb the day of Don's birth, I do remember thinking he was very pretty. Most of us had dark features from our Native American relatives, paired with toasted skin, and black or dark brown hair. I look more European than the rest, with light hair to go with my blue eyes. Daddy's eyes were such a pure shade of cornflower blue that they almost looked violet. Wayne's eyes were black, and my eyes had a sky-blue hue. But when Don was born, his eyes matched Daddy's. I knew by the look of him, Don was certainly *ours,* but even more specifically, I felt like he was *mine.* I would stay with *my baby* every moment I could when we were little.

Days were full for Mama then. At barely three years old, I was just old enough to do a few things on my own: I could dress, feed, and most importantly *occupy myself* when Mama had to love on Baby Don or provide special care for Wayne. Memories from that time are fragmented. When I close my eyes, I can still see my distorted reflection in the shiny metal of Wayne's wheelchair. The smell of his rubber tires is in my nose as he reaches out to cushion my tiny hands between his larger ones. Sometimes, he holds Baby Don in his lap. Baby Don always smells like powder. I'm not sure when that changed—when he started to smell like other things, like shoes, and grass, and a hot day. But those happy smells will always be with me.

Being the only girl among brothers made me feel safe in the world. I was sandwiched between them —the littlest lady of the family until blue-eyed Brenda was born.

We were primed for Brenda's birth because the stray we'd taken in had had kittens first. I'd noticed that Big White Cat, our family pet, had gotten rather fat, but I didn't understand why her body was changing so much until my very pregnant Mama said, "She's going to have babies." I was so excited I clapped and squealed. I'd been told about kittens, but I'd never seen one in real life.

When Big White Cat went into labor, Daddy fixed a warm bed for her: old rags and newspapers in a box inside the closet. Not understanding any of it, I got ready for bed. Mama said, "When you get up in the morning, the kittens will be here in the box." I woke up the next morning and ran to the closet. There they were—lots of tiny white kittens. Mama got one out and let me hold it. Wayne was already up. He had two kittens on his lap.

Daddy smiled as he explained, "They are brothers and sisters, just like you, Wayne, and Don." I thought Mama was going to have kittens. And that's when he explained to me that we were going to get another one of *us*. Daddy said Mama would have to go away for a few days to have the baby, and that he hoped our new baby would like us.

Later, we went to the hospital, and there she was. She was small and squishy, like Don had been when he was little and new. But, we all agreed that she wasn't as cute as Don. Daddy said, "That's how you know she'll grow up to be a beautiful woman." Over time, Brenda did become more lovely. Daddy was never wrong.

As I snuggled with Mama in her hospital bed, I watched my little sister squirming and cooing in her arms in the bed. Wayne watched with the same awe and amusement. He'd parked his wheelchair on one side of her bed and hadn't moved, smiling as he watched the innocence of a new life, proudly knowing he had one more sibling to teach and protect. I couldn't keep my eyes off Brenda—I wondered what it would be like when she was bigger, and we could play pretend in a *girl way* instead of the way I'd always played with my brothers.

That day, as Mama nursed Baby Brenda, Daddy got a phone call at the hospital. I could tell something was terribly wrong because of his face. His eyes widened and looked strange—there was an emotion I couldn't read. He looked disoriented and pale. Mama asked what was wrong. He put his hand up, shook his head, and rushed out of the room. The assisting nurses entered simultaneously and distracted us from whatever trouble existed outside the hospital room. Hours melted together as we fell more in love with the pink sleeping baby that was now ours—until Daddy came back for us, and time stopped.

When Daddy stepped back into the room, he seemed to be a physically different person. It was as though he'd been in a war, marked by age, grime, and weariness. He looked awful. His clothes were dirty, and he had a strange smell about him. His face was oily and smeared with black marks. Solemnly, he asked Wayne and me to leave the room. The nurses gently took our hands and led us into the hallway where we watched our parents through small glass panels in the door.

Daddy stepped close to Mama, gently holding onto her shoulders as he spoke. Mama's upper body went limp with agony, and she started to weep over sleeping Brenda. That is my first memory of overwhelming fear and seeing my parents' powerlessness. Mama had just given birth—and was now in a mental and emotional labor unlike any distress I'd ever seen.

The earlier call had come from a frantic neighbor alerting Daddy that our house had burned to the ground. The same good-hearted neighbor had gone over to our house while we were at the hospital to iron my family's clothes so Mama would have one less thing to worry about. But sadly, she'd left the iron on top of the ironing board, and it had somehow fallen over and set the house on fire.

Outside in the hallway, Wayne and I could only watch, wondering what had happened to turn such a happy day into such a sad one. Daddy comforted Mama as best he could until the dark, navy sky was so thick outside the hospital windows we had to leave. It was way past bedtime. Mama and Brenda stayed in the hospital, while we went to stay with relatives. A few days later, Daddy picked us up, and we all went to collect Mama and Brenda from the hospital.

As we walked through the long corridors of the hospital, we said little. Daddy's energy was so low it felt like we were trudging through the longest night to get outside. Feebly, he opened the car door for us and we climbed in. Through tears he tried to tell us what we were returning to. He tried to warn us what our little eyes would see; that it would be scary. But he wasn't composed enough for us to understand.

He used words like *iron, burned,* and *ash.*

When we pulled up into the driveway—there was a pile of black wood and charred furniture, the skeleton of a house we once knew. I could make out the shape of some things: my parents' bedframe, the legs of the kitchen table, and our wheelbarrow. Daddy said anything that could have been salvageable had been stolen.

Instead of doing what they could to help, other neighbors had come over to steal what was left of our family's meat and anything else they could carry out of the rubble that hadn't been charred or melted. Mama and Daddy had grown, picked, prepared, and canned many jars of food that were stored in a little building behind the house. Those were gone, too. In a poorer-than-poor community, you're only friendly neighbors until there's an opportunity to acquire "free goods"—even if it's due to another family's loss.

We had nothing left, except for Big White Cat, who had miraculously survived. Everything else *was gone.*

From L to R: Don, Gail, Wayne, Daddy, and Brenda

Without the four walls of our little house, we managed to find lodging for the next few days with Daddy's relatives who lived nearby. Later that week, the government stepped in and moved us to Steenson Hollow, where they gave us a little white house on the water. It was so much bigger and even had a bathroom with a bathtub. We were able to bring Big White Cat with us.

It was new and exciting, but sad at the same time, because of all the things that had been burned in the fire or stolen. I began to reflect on the memories I'd had in that little house, and how confusing it felt to have nothing familiar to return to when I was at my most exhausted. The safe feeling I'd had coming home after playing outside all day was what I imagined Daddy felt after returning from work. One memory saturated my mind specifically.

Earlier that spring, I'd been out all day with Wayne, playing with tobacco sacks. We didn't have many toys, so we used whatever we could find outdoors to ignite our imaginations. Mama was watching us—but only intermittently. She was patient while we collected little rocks in the road, accumulating the most beautifully marked of the bunch to save for later. Then we got rowdy with the rocks. Mama hated it when we'd get rowdy. I'd roll mine to Wayne—then he'd roll them back to me. I took the same form as when Daddy and I would skip rocks on the lake, and watch mine skid as Don hopped, screamed, and eventually wailed when he got hit. The longer we played, the more aggressive and loud our *fun* became, until Mama had reached her limit.

Enough! She called to us.

But we would not listen. We were in the heat of competition, past the point of composure. Until finally, I felt what I'd never experienced from Mama before—a unique punishment, in the form of a *whack!*

Dizzily I looked up at her. Over my head, she was wielding a flyswatter with an angry look on her face. The swat was one thing—but the look of disappointment and fury on her face hurt my heart. Mama had always been gentle with us, even when she was upset. I'd never experienced this side of her. Big tears welled up in my eyes. I cried and cried, and I couldn't stop crying. Then Mama started crying too.

By the time we made it back in the house, guilt had set in. She felt so bad about it she wrapped me up in her arms, holding and rocking me until finally she carried me to my room and put me to bed. But I couldn't sleep through the sniffling. A few hours later, I felt Daddy's warm presence enter the house, and I heard mumbling downstairs. She explained what had happened, and soon I heard heavy footsteps. Daddy's silhouette entered my dark room. He sat on the bed next to me. He wrapped me up in his arms and comforted me. I told him I was afraid of the next morning because I didn't know if Mama was going to be mad at me.

"Will she hit me again?" I asked him. I felt the heaviness and grief in his body when he responded, "No, Baby. Mama just had a bad day, okay?" I nodded as he said this, letting the fear dissipate. If Daddy said it, I knew it was true.

I stayed awake a long time after he left my bedside. After everyone had gone to sleep, I slipped out of bed to do my nightly ritual, despite feeling rattled by the day. My tiny bare feet tiptoed across the cold floor as I opened my creaking bedroom door. I neared the staircase and flipped on the warm light to herald two individual portraits in golden round frames that hung next to the bathroom.

"Goodnight Daddy," I said, looking at the picture of my hero.

"Goodnight Mama . . . I'm sorry," I whispered under my breath, before returning to bed.

Within six months I would be without a bed, without those two perfect portraits that kept us safe while we were sleeping.

Chapter 3

Steenson Hollow

"The best and most beautiful things in the world cannot be seen or even touched—they must be felt with the heart."
—Helen Keller

One day, *Little Girl's* Mama has to go to the hospital. Their neighbor tells her Daddy congratulations.

Everyone enters Mama's room after labor;

They *ooh* and *ah* over *Baby Sis.*

"She's ugly," the siblings say—

Even *Big Brother,* who only ever says kind things.

Daddy says this is a sign she will be beautiful.

Little Girl laughs—

And everyone is happy.

I was four years old, the day was clear, and I was too near the water. I knew better. Mama called my name several times, but I was having fun, so I stayed hidden there a little longer. In the distance, I could see our porch. Mama was standing there, checking on her four children to make sure we were safe.

I loved the way the morning sunlight would reflect on the ripples of the water, and the way the lights of boats would illuminate my bedroom at night. Everything was perfect except for the smell—floating fish, muck, and debris stagnated along the bank. The murky waters were filled with foreign treasures—but also brimming with scary turtles. Mama didn't like us playing in it. If we asked to play outside, she'd say, "Go ask your Daddy," hoping we would avoid the lake.

On one of our best days as a family, Daddy announced we were going to the *other side of the lake* for a picnic. My whole body felt elated as I digested the words I'd been longing to hear. *A trip to the other side of the lake?* I wanted to scream and laugh. To hug. To jump. To hurry. I was excited and admittedly a little scared to experience the lake I'd known for a year, but in a new way.

Daddy didn't have to ask twice to get us all quickly loaded into the car. My two younger siblings, Brenda and Donald, were still small—one and two years old (when Brenda was born Don was thirteen months old). My older brother Wayne waited eagerly as Daddy placed him in the backseat beside me. As we drove past the dock ramp, we came across a spouting spring where the water met the lake. It was the most breathtaking thing I'd ever seen.

When we stepped out of the car, Daddy unloaded planks of wood for us to walk on, so we didn't fall into the water or get our shoes muddy. He escorted Mama, then held my hand and walked me across the makeshift wooden bridge. He called me his *little lady,* his nickname for me, and I felt so loved and proud. Then he assisted Don and Brenda. Wayne was more difficult. So, Daddy wrapped him up and carried him, then went back to get the wheelchair, cradling it with the same care.

After we got across the spring, we knew we had it made. *This! This was the other side of the lake.* When I was older, I realized that the other side of the lake was just around the edge of the property a little way. But in my childhood mind, it was far away—a wild and wonderful place. The grass seemed far too tall to play in, but I did anyway.

Daddy and Mama put a quilt on the ground so we could all sit together. She managed the babies while Daddy pushed Wayne to our location as Wayne held cardboard boxes of food on his lap. Soon we were eating baloney sandwiches, and in that moment, it was the best sandwich I had ever tasted.

Donald Champion at two years old

After lunch, I ran free but close by, taking it all in, never venturing too far away from my family. I felt wild, fearless, and older somehow. Daddy played with us for a long time, until I asked if he would take me a little farther around the water. He agreed, then we walked, hand in hand, though never far enough for my liking. I wanted to explore the whole world with Daddy, even if my whole world was no more than a couple square miles.

In the afternoon, we all napped. Mama leaned against a tree holding the babies. Full of salty potato chips and sun, rest didn't sound like a bad idea. I don't remember dozing off, but I do remember waking up, stiff, sore, and painted red like a lobster. Despite my discomfort, I wanted to stay and play some more. But Mama and Daddy said it was time to go back home.

Loading the car to leave took a lifetime. As we left, I soaked up every last second that I could. I stared and stared, memorizing *the other side of the lake,* and I pretended it memorized me.

It was the first and last time we ever saw the other side of the lake.

Chapter 4

Daddy

"The most important thing a father can do for his children is to love their mother."
—Henry Ward Beecher

Daddy had the most beautiful eyes. They were steely and pensive—like Elizabeth Taylor's, primarily dreamy with flashes of melancholy. I'd grown up studying the thin sparkles of lavender that would sometimes appear when the light hit his face just right, envying his beautiful eyes and wishing mine looked like his. My irises were a unique swath of winter blue. They were frosty, clear, and bright—but not a deep well, like Daddy's. You could see to the bottom of his gaze, in more emotional moments it made my breath catch, even when I was a tiny child.

Growing up, I believed Daddy held the whole sun inside him; he radiated warmth, and an adventure seemed to always be building beneath the surface of his chest. Despite the moments of deep sadness that would occasionally show on his face, he kept a steady, positive outlook, which was saying a lot, since his childhood had been anything but easy.

Daddy walked with a bad limp and wore a special boot that was different from his other shoe. I asked him what happened to his foot. He said he hurt it when he was young, but he never elaborated.

When he was only fourteen, he ran away from home to escape his mother's abusive grasp. He joined a lumberjack company where he helped do the cooking until he was old enough to get a job as a cook in a restaurant. He spent his early life cooking here and there.

Over the next few years, with ambition and youth on his side, life took a really good turn for him. He set out to work hard and survive in any way he could—even if the odds were stacked against him. Free to live on his own without worrying whether he'd get yelled at or hit for no reason, Daddy developed a sense of calm. He believed in soaking up the moment and being grateful for all it had to offer.

This made him especially good with people. When he was in conversation with a person, he patiently listened to all their thoughts, dreams, fears, and pain. People mattered to Daddy. And in return, Daddy was well liked by everyone he met.

His creative side carried over from his younger years. He loved to sing and play music. He could usher us into a comfortable and tender mood with something as simple as whistling while making morning eggs. He was the perfect balance of peaceful and passionate, and made everyone feel safe, even in their messiest moments.

I suspect that's why Mama fell in love with him.

Mary June Meeks Champion and Emmett Abner Champion

Mama was only eighteen when she met Daddy. She was a senior in high school, and he was thirty-one. It was love at first sight. Back then, it was common for young women to move from their father's houses right into their husband's. Though Daddy had no money, he had a wealth of character and a deep reservoir of love for Mama. He was entirely devoted to her. And, certain that she was his forever, he wanted to buy her the perfect ring.

Unfortunately, times were hard. Very hard. The small town they lived in took a major economic hit from the Great Depression. Blue-collar workers were desperate to find odd jobs to help feed their families. Positions were filled as soon as news about them spread by word of mouth.

Since he had agreed to wait until Mama finished high school to marry her, Daddy used the spring of her senior year to contemplate ways to make extra money. As fate would have it, a fair was scheduled to come through town with attractions that promised cash prizes. Having strength, skill, and height on his side (he was 6'7"), Daddy was confident he'd be a strong contender in any contest. Being young and desperate, he reasoned it was his most viable option.

After a night of piercing colorful balloons with darts, slinging a sledgehammer in the *Strongman* competition, and attempting to capture lard-covered pigs before the sound of the final bell, Daddy entered the *greased pole* competition.

In the middle of an old racetrack was a large wooden post anchored in the ground. Its smooth surface was made even more slippery by a thick coat of grease. At the top of the pole was a fifty-dollar bill, which was no small amount at the time. The money was enough to motivate Daddy to use all his physical strength to scale the pole.

Several had tried and slid back down the pole with their only try. Daddy was being cheered on as he got nearer the top. Finally, with all his strength and determination, he reached the top and retrieved the money. He allowed himself to slide easily down the pole.

After receiving his reward, he went straight to the jewelers to buy Mama the most delicate diamond ring.

They were married in 1938.

Mama never took the ring off, and she never upgraded.

Daddy had the unique ability to bond with people over what *they* loved, as opposed to what *he* loved. Though I had always been a water baby, I could never tell if my love of Steenson Hollow Lake in Muscle Shoals, Alabama, was because of him, or if it was born into me. Being on the dock made my whole body tingle with happiness. I was certain I really did *love the lake more* than he did, even if he'd planted the desire.

From my bedroom window, I could see the expanse of the lake that seemed to go on even past the horizon. I'd never been to the ocean. I wondered how far it could possibly stretch if our lake itself was that big. It didn't matter that it wasn't clean. When you're little, you're not deterred by things like sharp beer cans, sliced tires, and cigarette butts strewn across the shore. You ignore things—like the tiny, scary spiders scuttling between the crevices of rocks, the shadowy parts of the marina where turtles and frogs love to cool themselves in the hot summer, and blistering sunburns that boil your skin, stiffen your body, and make sleep miserable. Even now, the smell of fish takes me back to the stickiest days of late spring when I would rush to the lakeshore at any cost, no matter how many times I had to ask Mama the same pleading question: *Can I get in the water?*

After one long day, Daddy came home from work. If things hadn't gone well, or if he was tired, it always showed in his eyebrows, which furrowed deeply. He'd get quiet if he focused too long on the workday, but it never gave way to complaining.

In an effort to make him feel better—along with thinking I'd *finally* get my way—I took his hand and suggested we go to the lakeshore. I presented my *totally original* idea as though anticipation wasn't hanging on every word. He saw through to my intentions, chuckled at my young persuasions, and agreed—we would go to the lake together. I jumped up and down and clapped wildly, especially because it would be *just us*. I loved moments when it was just Daddy and me.

When we made our way down to the water, soft pinks, sunset orange, and the glistening ripples of the tide welcomed us. We decided on a secluded rocky area, with the intention of skipping stones in the water together. I'd seen Daddy do it before, but he'd never taught me how to do it. He'd casually pick up a stone, pull back his arm, then send it sliding and skipping over the smooth surface of the lake. In every spot it kissed the water, it left a small ring that would expand until it was out of sight. My siblings and I would squeal as the skipping stones scared creatures beneath the surface. Small brown fish would dart as we disturbed their peace.

Excitedly, I grabbed handfuls of small gray and black rocks. I cradled them in the bottom of my skirt, oblivious to their shape and density. As I scooped what I thought were perfect rocks, Daddy stood back and watched me, saying nothing. Then he gazed long at the ground, considering his options. He sorted his stones carefully, choosing some, pausing, and rejecting others. This puzzled me since I figured any old rock would do. While I hugged my bunch tightly into my chest, determined not to lose any, I watched Daddy intently to better understand his plan for his well-chosen rocks. His deliberate actions piqued my curiosity.

After a few silent moments, he shot me a *Hey, watch this* glance. Deliberately, he drew his arm back, posing so I could see the whole process, and then let go of the stone with majestic grace. It felt dreamlike, watching the rock as it left his hand. It broke through the warm-lit sky and still air, then gracefully made its beats across the water. It skipped in slow motion, then seemed to flutter a little before magically dipping below the dark surface of the lake, out of sight.

My blue eyes widened and blinked at Daddy. My mouth hung open in awe. I wanted to do that too!

As he reached for a second rock I was already bursting with anticipation. I simply *could not* watch again without participating!

"Daddy! Wait! Let me try! Show me how! Show me how!"

I released the hem of my skirt, dropping all the rocks I'd collected, and clumsily danced over them in his direction. I figured I didn't need mine anyway, because his were special—and he would teach me everything about them.

Before handing me a smooth skipping stone of my own, Daddy walked me through the motions. I thought his explanation would never stop. The one thing I could always count on was his desire to slow down when I was at peak excitement. Without fail, every time I was extremely excited, he always told me to take a breath.

"I got it! I got it, Dad! Let me show you!"

He laughed warmly and gave me one of the special rocks he'd selected. I was so wound up I wouldn't have been surprised if my rock reached the other side of the lake. I pulled my arm back, just like he had, stepped forward while swinging, and with all my might, released the special rock. The rock went high in the air instead of skipping on the water. I watched it as my mouth made a perfect *O*. I anticipated at least one skip as it fell—and then . . .

Clunk.

Clunk?

It didn't skip. Not even once. It just hit the water and disappeared. I suppose my disappointment showed because Daddy bent down, hugged me, and said my rock *made very good circles*. So, I stared into the circles until they were absorbed into the body of the lake, then practiced my skipping once more.

The only thing I loved more than skipping rocks with Daddy was the thought that I might someday learn to swim. Daddy was a phenomenal swimmer. He could hold his breath for what felt like forever.

"Never try this," he'd instruct jovially before doing a marvelous dive that my siblings and I would of course immediately want to try. Our hearts would race as he'd stay under the water for prolonged periods of time—disappearing, then reappearing, as we all reveled in it. Mama, the more practical of the two, would stay dry on the shore, standing watch over her babies, Don and Brenda. She'd watch Daddy in the distance as though she was falling in love with him all over again.

Because of Daddy, learning to swim was the most important thing on my to-do list as a young child. Mama warned me to never go near the water by myself. Both of them had decided they would teach me together *when the time was right.* I knew what that phrase meant. *Later* felt like hundreds of years to my young mind. Unless it was immediate, nothing was ever soon enough. So, at four years old, I decided I was going to take matters into my own hands.

I waited until Mama was taking care of my siblings. Once the afternoon chaos, mess-making, wailings, and long sighs had commenced, I slipped out the front door. I'd been quiet all day so as not to draw attention to myself. It worked because I could tell Mama's mind was not on me at all.

Tiptoeing long after I'd closed the door behind me, I crouched low so no one would see me. By the time I reached the lake, my heart was racing. Somehow, without my parents there, it looked so much bigger. A tinge of sadness surfaced that Daddy would not be there to cheer for me as I swam. But I would show him later. *This was just practice, after all.*

Other people were already swimming in the lake. It was never a problem to get someone to watch us children because there were so many ladies with children. Everyone watched others when needed.

I sheepishly made my way to the water and put my toe in. It was mid-spring and still cold outside. The water sent chills all over my body as goosebumps raised on my arms. Knowing Daddy's method full well, I decided to take the leap instead of edging my way in. So, I backed out of the water, made my way to a small ledge, and jumped.

Instantly there was icy water in my nose. Ice in my throat. Ice in my chest. *Oh no!* I thought to myself as I flailed for the surface of the water.

I made my way up pretty easily, and then—I swam. I don't know *how* I swam; perhaps it was just pure instinct or having watched Daddy all those times. But my limbs naturally began treading water. Then I postured myself the way Daddy always had to get himself to point A to point B. I paddled my feet as hard as I could and resisted the urge to plug my nose as water flooded my nostrils. It smelled and tasted murky—like dirt, fish, and sky.

After making it to a shallower part of the lake, I rooted my feet in the shifting earth. I coughed, shaking water out of my nose and ears until I finally regained my bearings. Then panic set in as I recognized a silhouette in the distance—*Mama*. I was fearful she was angry, but her expression shifted from horror to amusement as I crawled out of the water and walked toward her.

"Mama! I was swimming! Did you see? I was swimming!"

More impressed than she was angry, she asked if I could show her again. She stayed to play with me and coach me through what already seemed to be ingrained in my substance. Later, when Daddy got home, she took me out for an evening swim to show him what I could do. He threw his head back in laughter as I wiggled, splashed, played, and was the center of attention.

His steely blue eyes were captivated by *me* on that day, as he smiled at *how grown-up* I was becoming. That day, I was ten feet tall. Daddy wrapped me in his warm arms and carried me all the way home.

Chapter 5

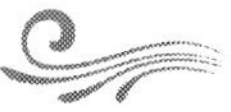

Family Photo

"Family, like branches in a tree, all grow in different directions, yet our roots remain as one."
—Anonymous

I look in the mirror and what do I see?
I see *Little Girl* at age three
Looking at me.
Little Girl is happy—
As happy as can be.

(Her family is poor, but she does not know it).

Little Girl has
Baby Brother
And *Baby Brenda*

And *Big Brother—*

Who she is certain is the best and smartest person she knows.

He has paralyzed legs, but can still crawl everywhere he goes—

But *Big Brother* doesn't seem to mind.

He makes the best of life.

She thinks he is wonderful.

Mama sweeps the floors and takes care of the children.

Daddy goes to work.

When he comes home—everyone gets hugs and kisses.

He laughs a lot and smells good after he has had a bath.

In the little house

At Steenson Hollow

Little Girl is happy.

There were two small stores across the street from the house where we lived. Being far away from other towns, their placement felt odd, but they provided endless entertainment. Both stores sold the same things, but for the sake of convenience, it made sense enough.

In each store there was a small refrigerated section with sliced cheese and off-brand baloney, a few cartons of milk, and the breakfast essentials. At most, there were two rows of dry goods. Because pancake mix was for special occasions, my eyes would always wander to it as we passed. My mouth would water, but I would say little, not always having the stamina to fight the usual response. *Not this time.*

At the back of both stores was what Daddy called the "odds and ends" section. It included a dusty medicine cabinet shelf, complete with gauze, spools of tape, toothpaste, and bobby pins. A rack of crossword puzzles on sale. A few pairs of oddly sized winter boots. Notebooks, crayons, and my favorite: toys. I'd save my bargaining energy for this part of the store.

Every now and then, I'd ask for something small and Daddy would concede.

"All right, just this time," he'd say in mock disappointment for giving in. The bargain was, I had to behave and maintain self-control after the purchase was made. I never held up my end of the deal, but Daddy reveled in seeing me happy. We'd exit as the jolly sound of the bell on the door of the shop would ring.

If one store was short of a vital item we needed, we'd venture to the other. They were so similar on the inside I got them confused. It was almost as if the ceiling panels housed the same damp corners. The same fluorescent bulbs were out on identical aisles, and the same musty smell of *old* permeated everything.

The one differentiating factor was the customer service. Daddy and I loved the store on the left because there was a lady there who laughed a lot. As she packed up our usual order of eggs, sausage, and fruit, she'd throw her head back laughing at Dad's silly jokes about the weather.

Sometimes I took a seat out front as Daddy packed up the groceries. The benches were usually open and we could watch the local children playing outside in the vacant alleyway. The light there always made our town feel like a classic movie set. It'd stream in and ricochet off the reflective shop windows and kiss the foliage of the tall trees that cradled everything. Even Daddy looked more alive when we were on outings. The morning trip to the store only took a few minutes but brought an excitement that filled the whole day.

Wayne, Gail, Don, and Brenda

Mama never went to the store. She would sometimes send Wayne and me to buy bread or something small. I was very fascinated about what was inside the store but didn't wander in just to look by myself. Sometimes I would walk across the street and sit on the bench to watch what was happening around me. Ladies going in and out. Men sitting on another bench, walking, smoking, and sometimes whittling on something.

On one occasion, I was sitting alone on one of those benches when I heard the lady who worked at the store on the left and another lady standing nearby cutting up, until they were both breathless with laughter. The conversation oscillated from thoughtful to funny to hysterical. Then I heard the store owner say, "I'll never forget this as long as I live!"

I had no idea what they were talking about at first, but their happiness made me happy. It felt like a treasure to be near a conversation with so much vitality, so I inched over in my seat to understand what was unforgettably impressive to the store owner.

As I got closer to the women, my face asked a question before my mouth did. "Do you remember?" I asked her, only moments after the subject had changed.

"Remember what?" The store owner asked.

"What you said you'd never forget!" I responded.

The lady smiled, glanced at the other one, then looked at me with a confused expression. I explained I'd overheard their conversation and quoted the store owner back to her. She said, "Oh honey, that's just an expression. I didn't mean that." They continued laughing while I tried to understand why anyone would say something they didn't mean.

Later that same day, I returned to the streets with my older brother Wayne to play with the children outside. Every adult looked out for every child as if they were their own. And yet, we were, for the most part, unsupervised. We usually stuck to the basics: bouncy balls, tag, bicycles, and cap guns. The cap guns were my favorite because I liked the way they smelled. I had accepted the fact that we didn't have one and I assumed it was because of money, but I never felt that I was *missing out*.

One boy who was bigger than the rest was often teased about his weight by a few bullies in the group. Thankfully, I don't remember any child being unkind to my siblings and me. This boy was especially kind to me, and gave the best cozy, kind hugs. He always shared his toys. One day he let me shoot his cap gun!

I was nervous when I pulled the trigger, even though I knew it wasn't a real gun. When my finger curled on the trigger, my shoulders got tense and raised up to my ears. I flinched at the noise that was scarier and louder than I thought it would be. After the initial surge of adrenaline, I soon found it was easy to pull the trigger. My eyebrows lifted as I looked at him, elated.

"It's sweet to let me play with your cap gun. Thank you for sharing," I told him. When I went to hand the toy back, he insisted on letting me play longer. He gave me more cap gun rolls and showed me how to make them pop. The grand finale right before he left us was hitting them with a rock. I'd never seen anything so fantastic! It was hard to pull me away after that, but Wayne looked at me and said, "Let's ask Daddy for our own."

I sighed, knowing it probably wouldn't be an option. But when we got home, Wayne headed up the conversation, and suddenly we were taking an *evening* stroll to the store, which rarely happened. There, Daddy bought us a box of crackers and a whole box of caps that Wayne and I intended to pop with rocks. Knowing we only had a certain amount, Wayne wanted to be careful with how many we used. But my hunger for the moment, like Daddy's, kept me plowing through them, making the most of every loud booming *pop!*

Onc day Daddy came home with what looked like sticks to me. I learned they were called reeds. Using his knife, he cut little holes in all of them. Soon he gave each of us one and taught us how to blow music from them. He called them flutes. We spent days playing them outside.

A cap gun with caps

On another occasion, while playing in the street, I blew up my first balloon. The same *Big Boy* gave it to me. I crinkled my nose, thinking the rubber smelled and tasted terrible. This was back when they dusted the insides with powder to keep them from sticking together. As I smacked my lips to get rid of the taste, the boy laughed.

While he could blow up a balloon with no problem, I couldn't get mine blown up. I assumed this was because I was *little*. The unspoken rule on the street was that the *big children* took care of the *little children.* All the *little children* were having trouble blowing up their balloons just like I was. Enter Wayne.

The beautiful thing about my brother Wayne was that he was always teaching me something. Wayne was a *big child* and so was *Big Boy.* So, they, along with the group, circled around me excitedly until my balloon began to expand in Wayne's care. Initially, when Wayne began stretching it, I squealed at him in protest, thinking it would break. He assured me, gently, that it was the proper way to blow up a balloon. After he blew it up to a grand size and tied off my gorgeous orange balloon, I trusted him all the more.

I have more pleasant memories than I can count from that little neighborhood. Once, when night was falling and the air had cooled, we encountered a tattered-looking dog that I immediately wanted to touch. Some of the children said, "Don't touch that dog, it has the mange."

I didn't know what that meant, but I did know that the dog looked pitiful, and I desperately wanted to help it. After determining the dog to be *old* and *disgusting* some of the boys got their cap guns and started shooting them in the dog's ears. The poor thing jumped and howled. I was so horrified and upset by it I began to tremble. Then suddenly, *Big Boy* took a noble stand and told them to stop. The disturbing "fun" came to a screeching halt, and I recognized *Big Boy's* ability to protect the people around him. While the other boys recoiled in shame, my heart swelled at the thought that I had *Big Boy* protecting me, even when my parents weren't around. This made Steenson Hollow an even more ideal place.

Gail at six years old

I was in first grade when I was told we were going to have photographs of ourselves taken at school. I didn't remember ever having my picture taken. I was giddy. I didn't have many clothes, but I was determined to go through them all to pick the perfect thing to wear.

Over breakfast, I told Daddy the big news. Though he was rushing off to work, he promised me the evening prior to picture day I would get a bath. He would help me get ready. Baths were few and far between in our home. Daddy tried his best to keep the bills manageable, so an evening in our galvanized metal bathtub was an event.

He told me once I settled on an outfit, he would use the bathwater to wash the outfit and would hang the pieces out to dry on the line. Excitement coursed through my body, and I got my wiggles out through the rest of breakfast.

I imagined what it would be like to hold a picture of myself in my hands, a glossy preservation of myself at my most beautiful moment. It made me feel special. When I tried to bring it up to the other children at school, they didn't seem to share my excitement. But by the time I got home, I was flying high. I waited with anticipation until the sound of Daddy's car made my ears perk up.

Anticipating I would be in such a state, he didn't make me wait. We headed to the tub in the yard. Once the tub was halfway full, I stepped in. The bottom half of my body relaxed into the warm basin, while chills covered my exposed chest and arms. Daddy gathered all the necessary supplies: a washrag, soap, and a piece of cloth to dry me.

"I have a special surprise," he told me, while popping open the cap on the shampoo. "We're going to wash your hair and do finger curls."

Finger curls?! I couldn't believe it! I was going to be *beautiful*. I knew little about the process, save that the curls required a ribbon. But when he went looking he was unable to find one.

"Well, I don't need a ribbon," he said. "I have just the thing!"

Knowing his ability to always resolve problems, I felt confident he would have a solution. Moments later, he returned with a shoestring from the shoe he didn't wear on his permanently injured foot, since he wore the boot on it instead.

Not only did I have the most gorgeous curls the next day, but Daddy took that same shoestring and tied my hair halfway up, and halfway down. A few hours later as we got our pictures made, my freshly cleaned favorite dress hung over my soft frame. And I still feel beautiful when I look at myself in that photo.

It was more than a photograph of me. It was a photograph of who Daddy was, and what he meant to me. He made me feel special to him that day.

Chapter 6

Mother's "Magic"

"Her children rise up and call her blessed; Her husband also, and he praises her."
—Proverbs 31:2

Mama seemed to have a magic all her own. It wasn't as charming and sparkly as Daddy's. Instead, it was sophisticated and practical. Mama had a way of enchanting the mundane. She could peel a potato or apple without the peel breaking once. My siblings and I would watch her as she prepared potatoes for lunch. We'd stand on our tiptoes, hovering over the kitchen counters wide-eyed, holding our breath as her slow, graceful mannerisms would carve something beautiful. She'd breathe softly—in and out, as though what she was doing was easy.

When the perfect peel of the fruit or spud would finally shake loose, we'd argue over who could examine it first. Don, Brenda, and I rarely trusted each other to *be careful* with something so delicate, but we all trusted Wayne. By the time one of Mama's pies was ready, she'd have several skins to pass between us. We never wanted to toss them out, especially if they were a vibrant red or green.

Brenda and I somehow outgrew our love for apple peels. When the Champion siblings visited me as adults, I always had apples. Brenda and I would peel ours, and Wayne and Don would go for the peels, saying it was the best part.

Mama made most of our clothes out of flour sacks. Even our quilts. Some neighbors didn't want the flour sacks and would give them to Mama. She also had a way of folding laundry that made us feel like we were *fancy*. She'd carefully tend to the few clothes we had by stacking them in identical flat squares.

She had a talent with the linens that Daddy did not. While making the bed, she could muscle the bottom sheet down tightly to the mattress, aligning the seams at every corner all by herself. She never asked for help because she didn't want help. We'd mess up her art form. I loved to watch her tuck our pillows beneath her tiny chin. Without being able to see where the pillow ended, she'd bring the pillowcase up flush against the bottom of it, release the pillow just a little bit, give the case a little shake—and *Voilà!* The pillow would rest perfectly inside.

We would always ask her to fluff our pillows and adjust our clothes. If she touched something, it became immediately more comfortable. We collectively agreed this wasn't just in our imaginations. This is why we loved it when she would dress us for special occasions. She could command a button, tie off a snag, and adjust a safety pin in any crisis.

The most amazing thing happened one day when we were all getting ready to visit Mamaw and Pawpaw. Mama had a ribbon she wanted to tie into a bow. She called me to her side and asked that I hold out two fingers, *just so*. Then, in some sort of magic trick, she wrapped the ribbon on my fingers, made some knots, then slipped it off my fingers. And there it was—a perfectly tight, glistening bow. When she put it in her hair, I was in awe of it. We'd always had so little, and yet she looked like royalty.

There was a natural elegance in the way she carried herself. She believed character and self-respect far outweighed anything that could be bought in stores, and this seemed to rub off on us even when we were tiny. We rarely felt *without,* even though we didn't have many store-bought toys to play with.

Once, when we were visiting Aunt Hazel, she made some clothespin dolls just for me.

Aunt Hazel was very fat. I followed her into a room to get the dolls. She decided to change clothes. I had never seen anything like what I saw when she pulled her dress off. She looked so huge it frightened me. I was horrified she would fall on me and crush me to death. I ran out of the room clutching my new clothespin dolls. They didn't have hair, but they had faces and tiny clothes on. I thought they were wonderful.

In our home, anything could be brought to life with a little imagination. Especially our kaleidoscope. It was, by far, the most extravagant item in our home—more of an entertainment piece than a toy. It was one of the *old-fashioned* ones, made of metal, etched with colorful designs that I could trace with my fingers. The vibrant beads would clink inside as we pointed it toward the light and twisted the end. Wayne taught me it was better to close one eye, if I could—but it was hard for me to learn how to wink at first, so I'd just cover my right eye with my hand while Daddy twisted the kaleidoscope for me. It was a family affair because it usually stayed put up unless we had permission to play with it while sitting on the couch or in bed with Mama and Daddy.

Afterward, the excitement of the moment would settle, and we would pack our fun away into its proper place on the shelf. It was *ours,* not mine—but I do believe I loved it the most. No one seemed to be as taken by the slow-moving colors as I was. I would press my face into it until my eye socket felt sore. I could hardly get enough. It provided play time that I could get lost inside of, and it was a singular experience. Every design I saw was private and unique. I'd never see the same combination of shapes and colors twice.

As a child, I only had one toy of my own—a tiny truck. In our shared stash, we all had that *one* toy we loved so dearly. Today I have a very beautiful kaleidoscope at my house. The grandchildren like to look at it, but they are never totally excited or entertained by it like I was.

There was nothing Wayne loved more than his marbles and knife. He also kept string in his pocket all the time. He could do neat things with that string; he'd gotten his skill from Mama. He would twist the string on his fingers and make what he called a "cup and saucer" or "duck's feet." Wayne also tied the string to his fishing pole. He loved to fish. He would slide out of his wheelchair and scoot to the edge of the roof of the boat dock almost every warm day and fish. It was good when he caught enough for the whole family. However, I didn't eat it because I didn't like the way it smelled.

We rarely played inside. We loved being outdoors. We played with whatever we could make an adventure out of: pieces of wood, sycamore balls, acorns, and rocks and sticks. Daddy's coined phrase was, "You children can make a toy out of anything." And I think, even if we'd had money, we probably would have been less delighted with having more. We'd inherited our parents' traits of wonder, imagination, and resourcefulness.

Sometimes when we'd open the door, Big Sloppy Dog would be on our porch. He was dirty and foreign, but he was as much *ours* as Big White Cat was. The boys loved him, and Brenda was somewhat amused, but she and I had always been far more fascinated with Big White Cat than Big Sloppy Dog. Being eye level with him made me dislike him. He was muscle, energy, sweat, and breath. I hated the way his sloppy tongue would hang out of his mouth and every now and then he'd steal a kiss right from our faces. He made me feel filthier than usual, and while we didn't live in filth, bath time was rare. So, taking a tumble with a large dirty animal was something I avoided.

As much of a tomboy as I was, I loved being a *girly girl,* and thus had a fascination with Mama's high oak dresser. I'd always been curious about what was at the top of it—it towered over all of us. As much as I wanted to know what great treasures sat on top, it seemed too special to even ask about. I was enamored by the mystery of not knowing, and somewhat feared the disappointment. One day, I finally asked Mama to let me stand on a chair and see. It was magnificent—like I was peering into a treasure chest. There was an ornate emerald hairbrush, a couple of decorative glass bottles, a jar of Pond's cold cream, and a two-piece bowl set that looked like a chicken (the bottom was its feathery fluff, and the top was its coiffed head and beak).

Mama's chicken bowl looked like this.

Naturally, I was curious to see what was inside the chicken. I was also curious about Mama's face cream. So, she pulled down the chicken and the Pond's. She told me to stand still while she smeared some of the floral-smelling lotion on my face. I noticed that the cold cream actually *felt* cold—even though the room was warm. Inside the chicken were pins, needles, thread, buttons, and a thimble; but then, these were Mama's magic tools. The only other thing that caught my eye was a glossy pink tube. Mama said it was called *lipstick*. I had never heard of it nor seen it before.

Carefully, she opened it while twisting the bottom. She showed me the rose-pink color inside and taught me to pucker my mouth as she applied it to her own perfectly shaped lips. Then she coated my lips with it and told me to smack them together. The lipstick also smelled good, and once I saw how pretty I looked in the mirror, I asked her if I could use it when we went to see her mother. She said *yes* and admitted that she had forgotten it was there. She, too, wanted to use it for something special—most likely a family dinner—because we never went out. It would be the perfect color for a night of homemade beans and cornbread, which Mama had been teaching me how to cook. I knew very little about the kitchen, but I wanted to be just like her. Daddy agreed it would be a good idea to start learning life skills, which included cooking.

Even fabric was too expensive for our budget, but Mama did make us some clothes while we were growing up. I loved to watch Mama as she took a flour sack, cut a few small pieces, and began to sew them together with a needle and thread. By night, one of us would have a dress or a shirt.

I was much too young to be safe with such treasures as scissors and needles. I'd examine the threads, knowing each one had been woven through the fabric with care. And each thread grew in significance as I aged because the threads aged too. As my body matured, the threads became softer. Some frayed at the ends, and I tended to them long after I'd outgrown the clothes, trying to preserve the work of Mama's hands and the memories of life before the sickness came.

Mama and her niece, Aunt Hazel's daughter

Chapter 7

Cancer

"Relying on God has to start all over every day as if nothing has yet been done."
—C. S. Lewis

Daddy knew that Mama didn't have long to live. On the day Mama left the hospital after Brenda was born, her doctor had diagnosed her with Hodgkin's Lymphoma. He said she might live 18 months with surgery. Despite brief spurts of recovery and terrifying declines throughout her treatment, Daddy was optimistic. He was confident in Mama's will to live because that's just who he was. After all, she wasn't really sick at first.

The symptoms were not noticed by me when she had all her strength and could make her way around the house, caring for the babies. I hadn't been told she was sick. She'd invited me to be the *big girl* when it came to Don and Brenda, to help as much as I could by bringing her diapers, assisting with bath time, and singing to my siblings in the soft glow of the light. Sometimes I sang to Mama too—Grand Ole Opry songs Daddy had taught me—when she no longer had the strength to put everyone to bed.

Though Daddy wanted to be with us every second, he had to go back to work. Mama had taken great care to groom me to be as helpful as possible—for myself, my siblings, and her, but I was only five years old. Knowing we'd need adults around, Daddy would have people come stay with us. Though I knew little about money at the time, I knew we couldn't afford to hire help. I suppose this was why there were so many different helpers. Occasionally our visitors were friends, but a few were women I'd never met. Some were White. Some were Black. Some we knew and others we didn't.

A Black lady I loved stayed with us the most. Wayne and I adored her teenage daughter whom she always kept in tow. The daughter's name was Beatrice. She had a bright imagination. This made her especially fun to play with. All day long we'd play hide-and-seek while her mother kept Mama hydrated and comfortable. We'd tuck ourselves away behind tree trunks and rocks, then yell, "Olly olly oxen free!" at the end of every game. Getting out of the stuffy house that smelled like Mama's sickness was good for us. Wayne would wheel out to the front porch to watch us chase and scream and topple over each other. He'd laugh hard, as if he were really getting something out of the game. It was the highlight of everyone's week when Beatrice came to play with us . . . that was, until *the accident.*

On our last day of adventure with Beatrice, we were playing chase, as usual. Our outdoor steps had a double rail. The lower rail was broken at the end, with a sharp, jagged point. As Beatrice mindlessly flung herself after Don and me, she ran, made a sharp turn at the bottom of the steps, caught the broken rail with her calf, and broke out in the scariest shrieks I'd ever heard. When we approached her, there was blood everywhere—the railing had ripped off a large piece of flesh. Her mother came running and was horrified at the sight of it. Even the neighbors heard and rushed to help, putting pressure on the wound and rushing her into the back seat of a car.

I was hyperventilating at the sight of my favorite friend being rushed off to the hospital. I was certain she was going to die, that I would never see her again, but Wayne promised me this wasn't the type of injury people die from. "The doctors can fix it," he said as confidently as any eight-year-old.

I figured Wayne knew the most about doctors, so I believed him, but I still waited fretfully to hear news about her recovery. A few days later, a bandaged but very much alive Beatrice stopped by with her mother and played with us for a while in the house, but not for long. Her mother was returning our house keys. She'd decided it was best if she *move on*. I hoped that maybe Beatrice would be allowed back to play with us again, even if only in the house, but she never was. The next week Beatrice's mother was replaced by Mary.

Mary was my favorite of Mama's caretakers. She was around near the end, when Mama was often too weak to get out of bed. I liked her a lot and learned that she lived in our neighborhood. Evidently, several of the people who helped us during that time lived nearby. The white people lived on the street in front of us, to the right. The Black people lived one block over and to the left of us. It seemed that only the people we didn't know stayed for a significant period of time. Daddy said they were *sent* and tried to explain they were from the Welfare Department and were on rotation to help Mama. While most of them were kind, one was absolutely terrible.

On one occasion, just as Daddy was leaving for work, a strange lady I did not recognize entered our home. She was mean looking, and I didn't want Daddy to leave after I saw her. We had a stool in the kitchen that we used like a highchair; Mama used it to put us up to the counter to eat. Daddy often sat on it, but we didn't use it much. With little warning, the woman sat me on the stool, fixed us something small to eat, and gave me some milk. Though Mama and Daddy had always encouraged me to clean my plate, they never forced me to eat or drink things I didn't like. My whole family knew I hated milk, so I was never forced to drink it.

I didn't like sitting on the stool. I couldn't get down by myself and was afraid I would fall, given its height and rickety legs. I cleaned my plate then asked to go play with the babies, but the woman wouldn't let me off the stool until I drank my milk. I tried to explain that Mama and Daddy never made me drink the stuff, but she wouldn't listen to me. I struggled to get out of my stool, but the more I pleaded, the more she resisted. Across the small room, I could see the pain in Wayne's face. It hurt him to see me being treated that way. He tried to help me by explaining it to her, but the woman would not relent.

I sat there so long my body started to hurt. My back first. Then my bottom. Then my legs. There was a rung on the stool, but it was far away from my feet. I stretched and stretched—attempting to give my straining legs a rest, but I was little and could not help myself. I struggled there for what must have been hours. But the lady would not let me get off the stool until I drank my milk.

By then I was sore and tired. I wondered if Mama could hear the commotion from the other room. I wondered if there was any way she could help me, but I never heard her call out my name. None of the other children were allowed to go in and tell her what was happening.

When the hand on the kitchen clock had gone all the way around a few times, I felt hungry once more. She would not give me any more food until I had drunk my milk.

I began to get sleepy, and I tried to rest my head on the counter, but it was hard to do without feeling like I was going to fall off. The more Wayne attempted to help me, the more he was reprimanded and instructed to stay outside with Don and Brenda. Though it seemed to be more of a punishment for my siblings (who had done nothing wrong), I longed to be outside too.

Finally, I heard the wonderful sound of Daddy's voice. It was one of the happiest minutes of my life. I started crying, probably uncontrollably by the way everyone was acting. Daddy got me off the stool and wrapped me up tight. I had been made to sit there for *over eight hours*. With zero hesitation, Wayne told on the woman. He spoke so rapidly and desperately he was out of breath within seconds.

Daddy was horrified by the account of how I'd been treated. I'd never seen him go into such a rage. He spoke assertively with the lady, then it escalated into an argument. They were both talking loudly. It scared me because I thought I was the cause of it. By that point, I was so desperately tired and hungry, I was just grateful to be off the stool.

After Daddy sent the woman away, I felt triumphant as he poured the terrible old glass of milk down the sink and made me dinner. After he put me to bed, he made a phone call for new assistance. He insisted the other lady be fired and requested someone be properly questioned and sent out as soon as possible. To our relief, that awful lady was the only terrible caretaker.

Emmett and June Champion (Daddy and Mama)

Throughout Mama's sickness, she and Wayne were often gone. Wayne was in the Shriner's hospital for children. Mama was in another hospital. Daddy's face had a sunken-in look, lines marked by laughter that rarely pulled back into a smile, unless it was intentional. He did however hug us longer and hold us a lot more—but it was different. Quiet. Soft. And melancholy. His joy came from us greeting him at the door while dinner simmered on the stove.

Stirring the bean pot was my favorite part of taking care of Mama. Though we had family nearby, none had come to help us when I first learned of her illness. Being her biggest, brightest girl, I was the first pick to help her while Daddy worked. She'd instruct me through ingredient lists, teach me how to turn on the stove, and how to prepare easy meals for breakfast, lunch, and supper. I was excited because I was finally just like her. I was practically a grown-up, handling dishes, using a chair to cook on the stove, and making sure to wash everything I'd used in the kitchen sink.

My favorite dish to make for Mama was pinto beans. She'd taught me that they were in the back corner of the highest cabinet. So, I used my best climbing skills to hoist myself from our stepstool to the cabinet, then I'd go up on my tippy-toes until my fingers grazed the bag. After retrieving the beans, I hopped down and approached her bedside. Together, we picked out the bad beans and the small rocks that were common in bags of beans during that time. Before preparing them to be washed and soaked, I retrieved one lucky white bean I'd been saving for Mama, a bean I had hoped would make her well. That was her trademark after all: add one bean to the mix of a different color, and never let anyone else stir the bean pot (otherwise Mama's magic would wear off).

Since Mama couldn't stir the bean pot, I was nervous. I told her I didn't think the lucky bean would work because I didn't have magical powers like her. She kissed my hands and assured me I did, saying it was the magic in herself and in Daddy that had made me. This realization made cooking for her all the more fun.

I soaked the beans for a little longer than Mama told me to and gathered all the supplies she'd told me, one by one. After adjusting the temperature of the pot just right, I poured them in, loving the rushing sound they made. Then, I added one cup of water at a time, and began using the salt Mama had carefully measured out beforehand. She said I was doing such a good job, she trusted me to follow directions for making cornbread. Though she doubted herself a few times throughout the process, and tried to lift herself up out of bed, she ended up being surprised by my dedication—and how delicious the cornbread turned out. I was growing up. I was five years old.

By the time Daddy arrived home with Wayne, Brenda, and Don, there was enough food for everyone. We gathered around the table without Mama, something I didn't realize would eventually become the norm. When Daddy served my plate, I got the lucky bean. Daddy took cautious bites at first, then with every spoonful afterward he made a *yum* sound.

"This is the most delicious they've ever been," he said with a genuine smile. I beamed with pride because Daddy never lied, and he was never wrong. No matter how bad some of my efforts surely tasted, he always made a big deal about eating them and brought a plate to Mama so she could taste my delicious cooking.

After supper, if Mama was feeling up to it, he'd take her on a car ride. Their neighborhood rides became less frequent as she got sicker. By the end, he was lifting her up in his sturdy arms, cradling her delicately, then gently placing her in the passenger seat. I'd seen him handle Wayne this way for the duration of his life. It seemed that no matter how big we were, Daddy held us all tenderly, burrowed in his chest, close to his heart.

Every now and then, Daddy would pick me up and cradle me too, before placing me in the cushioned back seat. Then we'd drive to a little store nearby to get a drink and a candy bar. These were our *special times* —before the numbness.

One morning, I noticed Mama's ring glistening in the soft light on her frail hand as Daddy held her palm in his. She'd always been tiny—5'2" in comparison to Daddy's 6'7" frame. But there was something about Daddy's presence that engulfed her that day—he was the sanctuary of safety that preserved her until the very end.

That night we had a particularly delicious dinner when Mama was able to help me cook from her bedside. I asked her if we could do it again the next day. She said *yes*, but we didn't. Daddy stayed home all day the next day to care for Mama. This was good because it was the same day Big White Cat died.

I wasn't even aware that she'd been sick. From the outside, she looked as normal, fluffy, and sprightly as ever. But when we'd gotten up that morning, Daddy announced that she was dead, out of the blue. To this day, I'm still not sure if Big White Cat truly died of natural causes or if Daddy saw what was coming and quickened the end to help prepare us for what was to come. Either way, her sudden absence, paired with Mama's sickness, affected everything. We were dealing with the encroaching presence of death in our own unique ways.

To show reverence to Big White Cat, Daddy suggested we have a proper funeral. He made a beautiful box lined with gorgeous cloth salvaged from some old clothes. While Mama napped, we went out and picked flowers for the burial. Then Daddy gently laid the cat in the box, and I cried. All of us cried.

Daddy had even invited a few neighbors to the funeral, which consisted of him digging the neatest little hole in our front yard, then nestling the beautiful box holding the cat in the soft earth. He then proceeded to gently place dirt on top of it with his shovel. I did not like that part at all. I was worried about Big White Cat, but Daddy said, "The cat's *dead* . . . this means she is at peace. She cannot feel anything. The worst part of the sickness is behind her."

It was the first time I'd ever been to a funeral, so I believed him. I closed my eyes, causing tears to stream down my cheeks, and tried to memorize what it felt like to hold Big White Cat, so I wouldn't forget. I cried harder at the idea that I would never cuddle her again. I would never touch her soft ears or tail. I would never have an afternoon nap with her curled up near my stomach. She hadn't even been gone a full day and I already missed her more than I could stand.

After Daddy fully covered the box, we took turns putting flowers on the newly formed grave. Daddy talked and prayed. He wept hard, almost harder than us. I hadn't known how much he must have loved Big White Cat to cry so many tears. Some of our neighbors led us in gentle songs and wrapped us up in big hugs. As we left the graveside, I looked at Daddy, hoping for an explanation. I was five years old and didn't understand so many things.

"Daddy, is there any way Big White Cat will ever come back?" I asked, hopeful that maybe the situation was reversible. Daddy shook his head, sadly saying *she would never come back*. I went to bed feeling wilted, wondering about all the moments Big White Cat had lived with us that I hadn't even noticed her living. She probably did all kinds of things when she was alone that I'd missed out on. I wish I'd been paying closer attention. I wish I could have loved her more, and for more days.

The next morning, dawn streamed in through my bedroom window. Having no curtains, I was an early riser, because the light always woke me. I tiptoed downstairs, edging past the bedrooms with doors still shut. There was a still quiet that covered everything—it felt wrong to break it. As I rounded the corner, fully prepared to *make my own* breakfast, I was surprised to see Wayne was already up.

He looked disoriented, and his face was blank. I'd never seen him look like that before. He looked up at me and said, "Gail, Mama is dead."

Dead. I thought to myself—entirely confused.

Dead.

At peace.

Dead, like Big White Cat.

I thought.

Then it hit me, and the pervasive heaviness that'd been hovering over our home for weeks broke like a downpour over our heads.

"*Dead.* Never coming back," I said wide-eyed, horrified at our new truth.

I looked at Wayne in a complete daze as he repeated himself.

Dead.

Dead.

Dead.

Everything was still. Warm light streamed in from the kitchen window, staining the dining room table where only one evening prior we'd sat as a family after Big White Cat's funeral—with Mama in the other room, sleeping and *alive.* Which meant at some point during the night, she'd slipped out of the pain of her own skin, and her soul had diffused over us, circulating through the house while we slept, like mystical dust. Into the dark she went, possibly through the back door which never fully closed, or a cracked window, or up through the chimney into the night air.

I suppose sadness was the third emotion I felt, right after confusion, which had followed a holy pause . . . a nearly imperceptible sigh of *relief*. This release heightened my sensations, making everything around me more *real* than it ever had been. The fabric of Mama's beautiful flowery pink curtains must have had a million threads. Suddenly they were all I could see. The *drip dripping* of our leaky faucet was all I could hear. The smell of Daddy's flannel shirt—his aftershave, was all I could smell. And that's how I remember Mama.

In the doorway, our neighbor heaved and wept. Wayne's eyes were bloodshot and weary. My initial shock—which he read as a lack of emotion—made him mad at me, first throughout the morning—then for longer.

My eyes landed on the stove. Realizing Mama would never prepare a meal for us again, I asked, "Who is going to make breakfast?" The question hung in the still air between Wayne and me.

"You don't care," he said, scoffing and shaking his head, as though he was learning something bad about me that astounded him. When I opened my mouth to plead my case, no words came out. I cared so much I couldn't articulate it. It felt as though if I spoke it, I'd be taken under by the wave of grief that was constantly constraining my breath and keeping my chest tight. Mama meant more to me than my five-and-a-half-year-old body could hold, so I pressed my whole body into Daddy and let the moments meld together.

People began arriving at our house from every direction. Some of them I'd never met before. Mama made a profound impact on everyone. Daddy roamed among them like a ghost, talking to everyone, but his eyes looked glassy and dark, and his spirit felt far away. I longed so desperately to connect with him. I wanted him to come talk to me so I could make *him* feel safe.

The smell of food, especially turnip greens my Aunt Dovie had made the day before, wafted through the house, and random strangers milled around a table full of food. Then I watched one woman whom I did not know come up to Daddy to say something. In a moment, he broke down and began to weep with his head in his hands. I'd never heard Daddy cry like that before. It was an infinitely deeper pain than when he'd told us about our house burning, or when he cried for Big White Cat not twenty-four hours before. The sobs racking his body kindled an inexplicable, protective anger in me that I couldn't control.

Thinking the woman had said something unkind to Daddy, I lunged at her and began kicking her. I'd never been a violent child, not even when Don would lose a game of tag and try to roughhouse with me. But feeling my shoes sink into the woman's soft, nylon-covered legs made me feel both vicious and vindicated.

Suddenly, there were large arms all around me; grown-ups pulling at me as I clawed at the woman. I aimed to ruin her hair, her necklace, or her delicate dress. Daddy lunged in to get me, worried more about me than anything. He'd never seen me react so aggressively. He put his large, gentle hands on my tear-streaked face and said, "Honey, she was saying something sweet about Mama. I miss her terribly . . ."

Even as Daddy's face became flushed and twisted with anguish, he used a handkerchief to dab my sore cheeks and raw, runny nose. He gave me a moment to collect myself before encouraging me to the tell the woman—who was most likely a relative—that I was sorry. I did, and she wrapped me up in a hug, and my whole body relaxed. Though it was confusing to let a strange woman hold me, I breathed in her perfume and rested my head against her shoulder. She would be the first of many foreign faces, and a far more compassionate source of comfort than what was to come.

Chapter 8

Mama's Funeral

"Losing a mother doesn't happen in a moment.
It takes years to appreciate the impact of what's gone."
—Lisa-Jo Baker

Mama's funeral was a terrible day. I was five and a half years old. It was 1948. We gathered inside a church with guests in dark clothing who smelled like coffee and peppermint.

Wayne told me, "Today, Mama will be buried."

Buried. In a box. Like Big White Cat.

Daddy had taken the time to explain the process to me. But there were still so many things I didn't understand or feel comfortable with. I had never seen so many people crowded into one space before. They were too close. They were bustling past us, yanking, pushing, and pulling us, wrapping us up in big embraces we never asked for, and saying *nice* things about Mama, when it was clear they never really knew her.

I kept being traded between adults. One would grab my hand, tug me around for a while, then leave me with someone else who would do the same. Some would cling to me until my bones hurt—holding me so closely I thought I might not be able to breathe again. Mainly, I was worried about my legs. I thought they might fall right off me. I didn't want to wrap them around people I didn't want to be holding me in the first place, so they just dangled there. Sometimes people would sling me from side to side, and my legs would swing back and forth. I wished I could just put them on the floor.

I tried to keep an eye on Don and Brenda. It's what Mama would have done. They were being passed around too, and I could see the distress in their young, scared faces. Though Wayne was older, everyone took liberties with his wheelchair. These were the times his handicap proved to be convenient. He could be passed about in his own way.

If I couldn't find Daddy in the crowd, Wayne was my secondary safe spot. But he seemed to be grasping for safety too, while in conversation with two people: Mama's parents. We had visited them a few times, but not often enough to have developed a close relationship. I supposed Mama had to come from somewhere, and she did kind of look like them both. They had the physical attributes of Mama, but they looked more like vacant houses—there was no light in them, no warmth. Years later, Daddy told me that their youngest son Raymond had just been killed in the war, a few weeks before Mama died.

Guests would stand still in front of the open casket that held Mama's lifeless body. I knew she was *in there* and I could have seen the form of her if I'd stood on my tiptoes, but I didn't want to look. I didn't want any other memory of her beautiful face than what I'd known at home.

The ominous presence of the casket alone felt heavy, and kept my breath caught in my chest and throat all day.

Everyone kept saying, "She looks so good."

"She looks so pretty!"

"They did such a good job!"

I didn't know who *they* were. But I had always known Mama to be pretty.

Finally, I was rotated to my grandmother, Mama's mother, Virtue Endora Basil Meeks. She insisted that despite my apprehensions, *I really did* want to see Mama, and *I really would* want to remember this. In slow motion she ushered me to the casket, hoisted me up with her thin, veiny arms, and encouraged me to open my eyes. My soft eyelashes blinked open to the sight of a white, doughy-looking body I didn't recognize. The makeup on its face was fully done—with a lipstick shade that *was not Mama's.*

"Mama?" I whispered under my breath. This was not Mama. After hovering in my grandmother's arms for what felt like an eternity, she said, "Now give her a kiss on the lips, Gail!" My body recoiled at her words, but she persisted. I told her no, but she wouldn't listen. So, she lowered me to the lifeless body beneath me, and I kissed the body's cheek instead. It was hard and cold. I hated it. It scared me. Even after I pulled away, it seemed as though the chill stayed on my lips for a long time. The sensation felt haunting, and I carried the coldness for days after.

I searched the room, hoping my eyes would meet Daddy's. I spotted the back of his head and ached for him to notice me. My gaze was broken by a young woman who lowered herself to my eye level. She was the first person to do this; most juggled me with little care about whether I felt safe. She held a pink gift bag in one hand, with white crinkly tissue paper sticking out of the top.

"Now, Gail, I have the perfect thing for you," she said warmly.

The gift was for me, which was as confusing as it was curious. I was somewhat excited, but my heart didn't flutter as I picked through the crinkled tissue paper, wondering what this stranger could have gotten for me. Nestled between the thin sheets of the transparent wrapping was *what felt like* a baby doll. I gasped as my fingers grazed her synthetic hair. Without even fully seeing her, I knew that she was beautiful.

The lady helped me pull the bag away as I tugged the doll out. She was breathtaking, with hand-painted rosy cheeks, dark brown hair, bright blue eyes, and long black eyelashes. I had never had a *real* doll before—only hand-me-down ones that were missing important parts, like arms or legs. My oldest one had a wilted eye; I kept her face down most of the time, because the open eye looked scary. Then, there were my *cloth* dolls which Mama had made from old pillowcases or handkerchiefs. I'd never had a new doll that smelled sweet like powder and packaging, complete with a cotton bib and ruffled dress.

I couldn't believe my eyes. I latched onto the woman's neck, and I latched onto the doll. Having the toy to occupy myself with while everyone offered our family condolences kept my mind off the line of people in front of Mama's casket. I curled up in the corner, tracing the curves on the polished shoes of my new friend; fixing her hair the way Daddy fixed mine. Some years later, I learned the lady was my second cousin, Olean, Gladys's daughter.

When my grandmother found me again, she saw my new gift and instructed me to put it in the casket with Mama, saying it would be the most appropriate to give to her, because she *needed something to take with her*. I felt sick as I reluctantly placed the doll beside the still body, while also being plagued with guilt that I *didn't want* to give Mama my doll to take with her. It didn't make sense to me. Why would she need it where she was going? Especially if being *buried* was as Daddy had described. Wasn't she already gone?

Virtue Endora Basil Meeks, Mama's mama

I searched the room for Daddy once more, confident he would resolve the issue. If only he would appear, he would tell my grandmother I didn't have to give my new doll away. I was internally screaming. Anger made my chest hot and my cheeks flushed. I stood beside Mama's coffin, baffled at what had just taken place, wishing *anyone* had seen what had happened and would be willing to speak on my behalf. But there was no one. There was only me—surrounded by eye-level, perfumy carnations.

I studied them closely. The small, creamy flowers should have been beautiful to me, but they made my stomach hurt. I felt lonely and isolated. I sought Wayne out in the church. He softened toward me as I sat next to him. Carnations instantly take me back to that day. I don't like them.

Around the same time, Daddy came over to join us. Despite the sorrow that weighed heavily on all of us, I was flooded with warmth at the sight of him. It was as though I hadn't seen him in days.

"Bring me my babies," Daddy said. So, they did. Just like that, the five of us were reunited once more. I was glad we were all together again. We'd felt fractured since Mama's death. On that church pew, we were able to sit and take one big, collective breath. Brenda and Don were sitting on Daddy's lap. I sat on one side of him and Wayne sat on the other. Together, we observed the long pause *after* Mama.

After only seconds, our break was interrupted. First, Brenda was picked up and placed on another row. I was *cute* and *little,* so I was certain I'd be next. My small fingers clung to Daddy's arm. As a man approached, he reached for Don and my heart sank. Away he went. I did not want to be away from Daddy—I resisted at all costs, and every muscle in my body clenched when one of my uncles asked, "Slim, do you want me to take her?" Before Daddy could respond, I involuntarily jumped off the bench and scooted in between his legs.

"No!" I cried, right as Daddy, in unison, gave the man a firm *no*.

Daddy held me close as my heart raced. Then a reverent hush came over the room, and everyone, including Wayne, dropped their heads.

Shhh . . . Daddy soothed me, nodding for me to put my head down too. From the front of the room a short man in a nice suit murmured soft words about Mama. Then everyone rested in a long silence before the man said, *Amen*. And everyone reached for the green and gold hymnal books in front of them.

Nearby stood my cousin Perry. He was the only person in a sea of voices whose words I could make out. He was singing something about *home, sweet home*. The longer the song went on, the harder people cried. I'd never seen Daddy and Wayne so distraught. Big tears rolled down their faces. *I should be crying too,*

I thought. But it was like I didn't know how. I couldn't seem to turn on the crying, which I couldn't figure out. I was certainly just as sad as everyone else.

Some became theatrical in their tears, raising their arms up to the sky, or placing their hands over their chest and wailing. Then suddenly, one older woman startled us all by loudly proclaiming, *Ho, ho, ho, ho!* over and over again through choked tears. I wanted her to be quiet; I felt furious toward her as people patted her on the back, comforting her. I didn't even know who she was, so how could she have been so upset by Mama's death?

After a while, another man got up to talk and I put my head down, but Daddy said we weren't *praying,* only listening, and I didn't have to bow my head. As the man talked, I pictured my doll again and worried about her. I really wanted her back and wondered if someone might get her for me later. I didn't understand I would never get her back. Like Big White Cat—and Mama—she would be *buried* too.

As soon as the man concluded his stories, they closed Mama's casket. When they did, my whole body felt relief. I loved the sensation of everyone rising in unison—shuffling out of the church into the bright day, away from the flowers that, for whatever reason, guests were taking with them. They didn't smell as strong outside where I could breathe. In the parking lot, I was joined by Perry who picked me up as we made our way on foot to the nearby cemetery. Perry was the first adult I felt safe with except Daddy. I was happy he was holding me. He had a sense of ease about him that enveloped me.

In the distance, I watched a bunch of men pick up Mama's casket and carry her through the air without wheels or anything to help them. I couldn't believe it. I assumed she must be really heavy. I was afraid they might drop her. But they seemed to have little trouble getting her all the way out to the gravesite where everyone was gathering beneath a tent.

As we walked, I clung to Perry even tighter, digging my fingers into his shoulders and wrapping my leg around him, clinging to the only thing I had to hold. He was beautiful and warm—I liked looking into his kind eyes.

While we made our way to our seats, I asked him to make me a promise that he would sing at *my dying*. He said he would. Then we took our seats to watch them bury Mama and my doll.

I watched Daddy's face as Mama was lowered into the ground. He looked so devastated and fragile. I searched for the magic inside him that always seemed to reveal itself even in the most harrowing of circumstances. But there was no magic there. I longed for the hope that had been the thread binding our family together. I wished for time to go backward. There was only sadness, and the hollow touch of each other's hands as we adjusted—slowly. Painfully.

On that little plot of land, my family buried our final days of sanctity and wholeness as a unit. Our best days were laid to rest beneath our feet, as a bleakness greater than we could have ever imagined loomed over the months ahead.

As the adults sang hymns and spoke of church and Jesus, I realized I'd never heard of church before Mama died. I was surprised to later learn from Daddy that he and Mama had been church members. I wasn't entirely sure what that meant. All I knew is that people kept telling us Mama had gone to Heaven to be with God and *the angels*. I didn't know what *angels* were either, but the way people were describing *Heaven*, I assumed that it was a wonderful place. I supposed Mama was very happy there, and given her condition, was probably in less pain. The idea of Heaven also made me fairly content to die. I considered that going to be with Mama would be wonderful, except for knowing it would make Daddy very sad.

He'd already cried so much; I couldn't imagine how sad it would make him for me to die too. But the talk of Heaven was nice. It gave me hope. But when people would say she had gone to a better place, I had mixed emotions. It was a mixture of sadness and anger. I thought she had chosen to go there and felt we weren't good enough for her. I thought our place was wonderful.

After Mama died, I'd sometimes catch Daddy staring long into his half-empty morning coffee cup—contemplating how to make our lives full again. He chose optimism and resilience after an upbringing that all but beaten the life out of him.

A few days after Mama was buried, we had a *fleecy cloud* day. The white wisps above looked fluffy enough to hold in my hands. One of my aunts came to see us.

We watched them together. She told me that each of the *fleecy clouds* were *angels,* and that Mama was now one of them. We chose which one we thought was her. My aunt said I should look for her each time the clouds were bright and fluffy because those days were when God let the angels come out of the golden gates to look down on the ones they loved. She also told me to be helpful, good, and happy because that's what Mama wanted to see the most. This made me want to be profoundly good—for Daddy, for my siblings, and for her. I felt such peace knowing Mama was right there above me, and I could talk to her any time I felt sad.

For the next five years, although the world became very dark at times, the clouds preserved me. I would search the sky for Mama, then as soon as I spotted her, I would assure her everything was all right, even when things proved to be quite the opposite.

I was ten years old when I learned my aunt had told a *white lie* to me. That she'd made up the story about the clouds to make me feel better. The grief of that realization and everything it meant weighed heavy.

The sky was just the sky.

Clouds were just clouds.

Pretty soon, there was no Mama at all.

I longed so desperately to look up at the sky and say, "Don't you worry, Mama. Everything is just wonderful here. I really do mean it." Even if it meant I was *white lying* too.

Chapter 9

Away to Aunt Vertie's

"There is nothing permanent except change."
—Heraclitus

A few days after Mama's funeral in November, all our things were packed into boxes: the few clothes I had, Don's toys, Brenda's baby blanket, Wayne's medications. The grown-ups surrounding Daddy insisted he could not care for all four of us. Though Daddy was upstanding and had good intentions—they were right. We barely had the means, and there weren't enough rotating caretakers in the world to be able to manage the chaos and despair of our home. So, Daddy sent us away to the houses of separate family members. I was sent to Aunt

Vertie and Uncle Roy's house. Brenda and Don went to live with Daddy's sister, Aunt Dollie.

We grieved. We missed Mama. We felt hollow and above all things—confused.

Having just lost Mama, I initially found solace in the idea that if I couldn't have Mama, surely relatives (and specifically, her sister) would be the next best thing. I don't remember seeing her at Mama's funeral, but she was probably there. I tried to remember if Aunt Vertie smelled like her, had similar mannerisms, and hugged me like Mama did. I wondered if she'd have colorful stories about them growing up together, like the ones I had about Wayne, Brenda, and Don. I hoped to learn more about what Mama was like at my age.

Daddy's sadness permeated everything as we slowly rolled into the parking lot of the country store. Aunt Vertie and Uncle Roy's house was attached to the back. Elderly folks filed in and out of the front door of the store with their usual orders of over-the-counter medicines, hard candies, chewing gum (people always seemed to have chewing gum), and drinks in glass bottles. For an instant, my deep sorrow was eclipsed by a flicker of intrigue. It reminded me of the stores like the ones across the street from our old house, where the shop owners were friendly, the children played outdoors, and old men sat on the porch.

This might not be too bad, I thought to myself, as Daddy stopped the car. I eyed the silver-haired men in suspenders and friendly older women in crepe pastels, wondering if they would try to pull at me the way all the senior church members had at Mama's funeral. But when Daddy walked us through the shop to Aunt Vertie's front door, the worst the women did was *coo* at me while the men tipped their hats.

As we walked through the store, I eyed the rows of snacks in glistening packages: chocolate bars, brightly wrapped chips, a refrigerator full of beverages, gum in every flavor, and a shelf full of children's knick-knacks. My chest swelled with anticipation at the sight of a bouncy ball, a tiny jacks set, and a selection of coloring books. Out of respect to Daddy, I asked for nothing and redirected my attention ahead.

I'll come back and look at these later, I thought. I assumed Aunt Vertie had the run of the place, and there would be special treat times, just like Daddy had always given us. Little did I know my expectations would be drastically different.

After Aunt Vertie opened the door, my stomach sank. It would only take a moment to realize that there would be little to no special treats for a very, very long time.

Aunt Vertie's interactions with Daddy seemed cool and guarded. I wouldn't find out until much later in life that Daddy had been engaged to Aunt Vertie prior to falling in love with Mama, who was younger and much prettier. A woman scorned, Aunt Vertie never fully got over it, which is why I suppose she allowed her jealousy to get the best of her.

Her tone, which was stern with Daddy, would be even harsher with me. So, I stayed quiet and tried to stay out of her way. While I clung to the memory of Mama, I could tell Aunt Vertie was having an easier time with the loss of her once-beloved sister. Looking back now, she was likely annoyed and inconvenienced by my presence. After all, I looked like Mama. I was a constant reminder that Daddy hadn't chosen her.

"We just keep moving on," she noted often, in a removed tone that made her seem vacant of all emotions. Though my memories of her were slight at that point, I couldn't remember a time when Aunt Vertie visited that she'd ever been expressive about seeing Mama, or even my siblings and me, for that matter. "Your aunt and uncle are coming to visit," Mama and Daddy would say. But when they'd arrive and Aunt Vertie would crouch down to hug us, her face was expressionless.

Surely there was an excitement I was *supposed* to feel about her, but I could never seem to access it. She and my uncle usually brought us candy when they came to Steenson Hollow. Given our love for special treats, their trips should have felt happy. I came to learn over the years that it was never about the gifts and always about the giver. I would come to learn about the vacancy that lived inside of Aunt Vertie. It was a dark, all-consuming void.

The first thing I would come to understand was that Uncle Roy was a temperate man who lived in the wake of a tumultuous woman. I can only imagine what it would have been like for Uncle Roy to be married to Aunt Vertie, knowing that he wasn't her first choice either. While she could be verbally critical, her weapons of choice for Uncle Roy were calculated manipulation and cold silence. His response was just to survive the chaos of Aunt Vertie's hostile temperament.

From the moment I stepped over the threshold of her house, Aunt Vertie made it her goal to get even with Mama. Instead of choosing to relish in *being picked* by a husband who clearly loved her, she wanted retribution for Daddy's actions, and thus was not kind to me. Their children basically ignored me. And although Uncle Roy always treated me well, he was in the store all day. I barely saw him in the house part of the structure. This was due in part to Aunt Vertie's passive-aggressive behavior toward him.

The shadowy house had a long hallway with doors to several rooms. Each of their three children had their own space, which was a new concept for me; my siblings and I had gotten used to living in close quarters. I was allowed in the bathroom, the first door on the left in the hall. But I was not allowed in the bedrooms. They were private spaces, *for family members only,* and although I was family by blood, I was a foreigner in her eyes. I was only allowed in the common places, and even there it was better that I was *out of sight and out of mind.* I never went to the end of the hall. I only saw there were doors that family went in and out of.

In turn, I'd make myself a space wherever Aunt Vertie was not. This meant that except for mealtimes, I was usually in the kitchen, which had buttermilk yellow cabinets, old black-and-white tile, and a table long enough to serve the guests they occasionally invited over for show. There was also a darkly lit living room which housed a forest green sofa, an orange and crimson floral chair, and a dark wood coffee table that faced a fireplace.

And that's where they made room for me.

My "room" consisted of the ten square feet in front of the fireplace. The pallet I slept on was hardly a pallet. It was four tattered blankets—not even warm enough to protect against the relentless winter outside—laid beside the stone hearth. By day, it was taken up and stowed away in the linen closet—as if I wasn't there at all. At least it was close to the bathroom, which was at the start of the hallway.

Though blankets were few, and warm winter clothing was nonexistent, I felt lucky every time the fire was blazing. Aunt Vertie kept the embers lit for the duration of the cold months. I could find solace in drifting off to sleep every night to the hot flicker of glowing ash. When night would fall and the ache for Mama and Daddy would overcome me, I'd focus on feeling the heat on my face and imagine I was back at the old house, blowing kisses to my parents' photographs before crawling into my cozy bed. I'd gone from having two people who loved me, tucking me in each night, to waiting until everyone was ready to turn in to finally rest my weary body.

I rarely cried during the day. That felt too vulnerable. So, I'd let my pillowcase cradle my sadness in the night, holding what I couldn't show while I was awake. This usually resulted in me drifting in the space between sleep and wakefulness, a state worsened by the fact that Aunt Vertie's house was very close to the railroad tracks.

Though I liked watching the train during the day —and I'd often wondered where it had been and where it was going—I didn't like it at night. It roared, steamed, and made terrifying screeches that sounded haunting and ominous at night. Because the house was only built over a crawlspace and not a solid foundation, the passing train would make the wood floor shake. As it barreled through the most delicate nights of my childhood, I was horrified it might derail and flatten the house with me in it. The more my fear increased, the closer the train sounded. No matter how many nights I heard the *ding* of the red-and-white crossing bars lifting, I was convinced the train was chasing me down.

I had nowhere to hide from my fears, so I would just lie there on the pallet. Sometimes my fingers would trace the wood floor. I'd fear that bugs or mice might make their way across my body in the middle of the night. Wayne had once told me a story about a spider crawling into someonc's car and laying eggs. So, I'd plug my fingers into my ears, hoping I could protect them from insects crawling inside. But by morning I'd wake up to find—to my horror—that my fingers were no longer protecting me.

Meanwhile, the rest of the family was in the *back of the house*. The back of the house stayed warm most of the time, whereas my spot in front of the fireplace was usually warm when I went to sleep, then cold by the break of dawn. When the winter cold would stir me awake, it was almost impossible to get warm enough to go back to sleep.

On those occasions, I was especially grateful for the family dog, Bennie, who would join me on my pallet and let me burrow my face, chest, and belly in his fur. Up until that point, I hadn't liked dogs. I didn't particularly like him sleeping with me then, but I knew I'd freeze otherwise. Nestled in his black, scrappy coat, I'd longingly stare up at the couch, imagining my icy toes plunged in between its thick cushions.

Aunt Vertie had caught me sleeping there once, and I'd gotten a tongue lashing. I once asked Aunt Vertie why I couldn't sleep on the couch.

"Couches are for sitting. Not for beds," she'd say.

Couches are for sitting.

Beds are for sleeping.

The floor is for you . . .

When I was awake, I was cleaning.

By the evenings, my hands would be covered in blisters from handling a broom that exhausted my five-year-old body with its weight and stiffness. While the other children, Eli, Isaiah, and their sister were in school or playing outside, I was forced to sweep. Every now and then the straw bristles would catch my freezing feet and scrape them just enough to make me let out a raw sob.

When Aunt Vertie would send the children out, she insisted they were *too old to enjoy playing with me,* and she'd have me clean. Then, she'd come in and look around—always with an expression of dissatisfaction, and demand I resweep the house, the store, and especially the front porch and steps.

Her children never swept. Every now and then I'd hear them outside giggling and playing. Their favorite game was *chase*—as mine had been with my brothers and sister. I couldn't understand why they were too old to play with me, especially if we loved the same things. I felt deflated constantly but learned to hide my emotions under Aunt Vertie's sharp watch.

Being criticized constantly made me feel like there were eyes in every corner. So, I was especially thankful to Uncle Roy when he would, in private moments, be kind to me. Every now and then he'd say a soft word, sneak me penny candy, or help me sweep. Even the old men on the porch would sneak me penny candy now and then because they knew Aunt Vertie wasn't treating me right. I loved chewing gum but Uncle Roy never gave me any. I guess he thought Aunt Vertie would know if she saw me chewing it. Candy could be eaten quickly.

On the few occasions Aunt Vertie caught her husband being kind to me, she'd viciously reprimand him. I got the sense that Uncle Roy thought the floors looked just fine. I suspected they were not even dirty, that she just wanted to inflict chores on me to exercise complete control.

While I was grateful for the special treats Uncle Roy would attempt to sneak me, what I really wanted was to be held. Sometimes, if I was upset enough, Uncle Roy would nestle me in his arms and whisper a sweet, "It's going to be okay." Even if I knew it wasn't, it felt so nice to hear a grown up say it. It'd been so long since I'd been cradled by an adult.

When he'd soothe me, I'd pretend his arms were Daddy's big, soft hugs. I'd picture Daddy carrying me: back home from the lake, up to my room when I was sleepy, or in from the car in rainy weather. When Uncle Roy would release me, I'd hold that feeling of being hugged until my head rested on my pillow at night. It was the only human contact I had to get me by. But if Aunt Vertie entered a nearby room, I would feel Uncle's arms immediately go slack—as though I was a delicate doll being placed back on the shelf, only to sit silently, no matter how alone I felt.

I didn't understand what was happening to me. I wondered if it was happening to my siblings. I didn't know why I was there or how long I would have to stay. I didn't know exactly why Daddy had given me away after Mama died. I was a miserable, starving, and dirty child.

Aunt Vertie, Brenda, Don, and a grandchild at Childhaven. I was out of town. Don and Brenda didn't remember seeing her before. To them, she was just Mama's sister.

Aunt Vertie was always stingy with food for me. Even though she could afford to feed me, she kept my belly growling. She also tallied up everything I ate: every bowl of soup, every carrot, every pea. I never understood this grandiose measure of control until much later in life, when I learned that she had been keeping a tab—totaling up my expenses to bill Daddy for my stay. I was aware that every breath I took was a burden to her. The smallest requests were treated with hostility and followed up by mean comments about me being a nuisance. My basic needs were *unrealistic*.

However, on one occasion, I was taken into the kitchen by Aunt Vertie to have my hair washed. She bathed me, something that had never happened. I hadn't been properly washed since before Mama's funeral, which could have been weeks or months before. Time crawled on. Afterward, she draped a pressed and clean dress over my shoulders, then put lacy white socks and shiny black shoes on my feet. Then we went to the porch and sat together in a white wicker chair. She propped me up on her very bony and uncomfortable knees, but never drew me near. Her perfume wafted around me, but it smelled too sweet and floral, nothing like Mama's scent of Ivory soap. We hardly exchanged words. The long silence was broken by cars coming and going. I paid little attention to them until one stopped, and a familiar silhouette stepped out in the distance.

Daddy!

With no hesitation, I jumped down and rushed to him. My heart was as light as air. I felt like a leaf flying in the wind when he picked me up. I cradled my head in his neck, and he held me there. His tears fell onto my forehead and mine soaked into his flannel shirt. I never wanted to let him go. He had come to get me. I couldn't believe it. My smile must have wrapped all the way around my head.

The men on the porch were happy to see us reconnecting. The sound of the wind chimes hanging from the store awning tinkled in the distance.

A happy song—*finally*.

Saying little, Aunt Vertie invited Daddy in. I was desperate to leave that place and hold Daddy's hand all the way to wherever we were going next.

Finally, the moment came for us to leave. He thanked Aunt Vertie and Uncle Roy for all they had done, then took my hand and led me out to the car. But I never got in.

Soon, Daddy broke down in tears, embraced me, and began to talk to me.

"Gail, I'm so sorry. I have not come to get you." He explained that he had only come for a visit. My heart, which had already been so fragile, absolutely broke. I wasn't sure what dying felt like, but I began crying hysterically, my small chest rising and falling as Daddy tried to comfort me. His brow was now furrowed as he tried to keep it together, but I was already past gone.

"I promise," he said, trying to console me. "Soon, I will come to get you for good, and all of us will finally be together."

Between panicked breaths and shocked tears, I savored the moment, feeling more desperate to hold it as Daddy moved closer to the car. Before he could get in, I clung to everything I could grasp: his coat, his belt, his legs. Moments later, as his car rolled away without me in it, I couldn't stop myself from chasing it. I leaped into the wind with all my might, thinking I could run fast enough to keep up with his car. Until finally, my legs gave out, and the car faded from sight. Defeated, exhausted, and debilitated from weeping, I slowly walked back to the house. I was changed. In that moment, I was no longer a child, but far from being a young woman. Instead, I was an old soul in a small, weary body.

The old men on the store porch looked genuinely sad for me. Some patted my shoulders as I walked by. After I stepped back inside the house, Aunt Vertie took the pretty dress and shoes off me and put my tattered clothes back on. At that moment, I decided that no matter what happened, I wasn't going to sweep anymore. No matter what she said or how many insults of disapproval she used, I would not raise a finger to clean for that woman.

Instead, I took to the porch. I would wake early, then go sit outside in front of passersby all morning, where Aunt Vertie *couldn't* be cruel to me. It was warm now. I loved feeling the sun on my body. I watched the road every day, waiting for Daddy to come back.

As I was sitting on the step one day, Aunt Vertie came to the front porch and announced, "This porch really needs to be swept."

I didn't look at her.

I didn't move.

I didn't sweep.

A few weeks later, Daddy returned for a visit. But it didn't feel as happy as the first time. By then, I was tired and delicate. All I wanted was for him to hold me for a long time. And he did. He told me that we would be seeing Brenda, Don, and Wayne, that he had a house all set up for us, and we were going there soon.

Years later, I asked Daddy why he had sent me to Aunt Vertie's. He said she'd asked for me. After I left, she sent Daddy a bill for fifty-six dollars, for the food I had eaten and for taking care of me. Daddy paid it in full.

Chapter 10

Moving into Mammy's House

"The LORD is my light and my salvation;
whom shall I fear?
The LORD is the stronghold of my life;
of whom shall I be afraid?"
—Psalm 27:12

Daddy took me from Aunt Vertie's. As we drove, just Daddy and me, the cool October air nipped my nose through the cracked window. Daddy turned up the heater. The smell of ripe apples felt like an appropriate *homecoming*. I wasn't sure what Daddy had in store for us. But every mile we ventured together meant more time absorbing

Daddy's presence, which I couldn't get enough of. To savor the moment, Daddy pulled off the road.

"We're almost there!" he said. I wiggled with excitement at the news. The narrow road that led through the woods was covered by piles of fading foliage. We followed a winding road through the woods for several minutes until a little wooden house suddenly came into view. When we arrived, Wayne, Don, and Brenda were already out in the yard. I clapped. I cried. I giggled. We wrapped each other up in hugs so deep they hurt, but we didn't loosen our grip.

Wayne held me forever; I celebrated the smell of his hair and put my hands on his soft cheeks. We immediately broke into a game of chase right before another car came in behind us. There was a woman in it. Her window was rolled down and she was throwing her hands in the air, yelling loudly at Daddy. His eyes widened in an expression I had seen on his face only a few times before: *complete terror.*

He approached her car door and kindly requested she speak with him privately. The car door slammed so loudly I covered my ears. A wash of anxiety overwhelmed me. Though I couldn't hear what they were saying, I knew they were both mad. They got louder until I was so afraid I began to cry. The arguing continued at deafening decibels until Daddy lifted his arm and struck her hard across the face. I covered my eyes but peeked through, horrified as she picked up a palm-sized rock and threw it at him.

I later learned that woman was his sister, Aunt Maddie, who was at least twice his age.

"You're a fool for bringing them here, knowing what kind of a woman she is!" She hysterically yelled.

I didn't have any idea who she was talking about or why she and Daddy would be having such a fight over another woman. Aunt Maddie and Daddy both knew something we didn't. But we'd find out soon enough.

The next thing I remember after Aunt Madie left was going inside the house. Mammy was in there. I was told who she was.

Daddy had run out of options. We were moving into Mammy's house.

Mammy

Aunt Maddie and Uncle Ben were the matriarch and patriarch of Tishomingo, Mississippi, which consisted primarily of their children and grandchildren. Maddie was the oldest of the three children. She had grown grandchildren by the time I was a small child. Her old house was a bungalow with a wraparound porch. It even had a well on the porch that sat beneath a round, castle-like tower. The house did not have indoor plumbing. But it didn't matter. She had children living around whose houses did.

Her daughter, Gladys, was a nervous woman. She was actually my cousin, but she was so much older that we called her "Aunt Gladys." She had lots of wrinkles on her forehead and around her mouth that made her look older than she really was. Over the years, she had several mental breakdowns. I believe these breakdowns were partly because of what happened to us—because of what Mammy did.

Aunt Gladys had married a man with more money than most people in the area. Her teenage daughters, Sadie and Joyce, were pure beauty. They were entirely lovely to me when I started school. Aunt Gladys had left a few dresses for me. I had shoes. There was no kindergarten back then, so I started into school very soon. Knowing I was smart, Daddy was confident I was ready for it.

I would walk through the woods to be picked up by the school bus. Wayne went with me at first. The trail was wide enough to fit his wheelchair with me strolling alongside him. Handicapped children like Wayne were not allowed to go to school. Years later, he said it was his biggest regret.

Those moments with Wayne were a time of real relief from Mammy's house. The school bus was filled with a lot of my cousins. It seemed like everybody in the entire area was our kin somehow. Even my aunts and cousins were the cafeteria ladies and always made sure I had something to eat.

I was the baby of the class, and this made playing outside *fun*. It was nice being the youngest and not having to take care of anyone. My older cousins would play with me like I was a toy—they'd swing me, toss me, and chase me, but would never hurt me. They'd take turns carrying me to the school's outhouse when I needed to go to the bathroom.

When I started first grade, I was the only child in first grade in the whole school. My teacher, Mrs. Short, was kind to me but very busy with grades that had more students. She never had time to teach me in one-on-one lessons.

"I'll get to you later, Gail!" she'd tell me. Then, she'd give me homework matching what the others had learned. I always felt like I was treading water, trying to teach myself the new material and not fall too far behind. Sometimes, this advanced curriculum worked in my favor. It exposed me to reading and math skills that I could occasionally grasp. But given my lack of a solid foundation in every subject, I had little to build on.

Though Daddy had always told me I was smart, the gap in my learning began to make me question myself. When I wasn't being given the same assignment as everyone else, Mrs. Short would ask me to do repetitive exercises that bored me. I'd find myself distracted and restless, staring out the window at the plush green grass and vibrant trees, wishing I could just go play.

Recess was my favorite part of school. We only had made-up games to play. Boys would play stick ball with a wadded-up piece of paper. We mostly ran and chased each other. The older children would play games with us.

It was hard to get the hang of a new school routine and new living situation at first, but it became somewhat easier over time. It was good to have their affection, because moving into Mammy's house changed all of us.

Adjusting to Mammy's lifestyle and personality was a wild, disturbing experience. I understood that Mammy had been incredibly cruel to her own children, so it made sense that she would be mean to her grandchildren. She never wanted any of us because she never wanted any of *them* to begin with. She didn't have the capacity for that kind of love.

Older people said Mammy had been beautiful once. But I was never able to see a stitch of attractiveness in the stories I'd heard about her because I was presented with her harsh temper from a strange woman.

There was neither warmth nor softness in Mammy. Her mouth never opened to smile or laugh, but then, there never seemed to be much to be joyful about. She had a deep anger in her and a permanently furrowed brow that made her appear as though she was always burdened by something. Though I was young, I sensed existing had always been hard for her and her expressions revealed decades of contempt, resentment, and sorrow.

I wondered if she'd ever felt glad before. I couldn't picture her relaxed. I also couldn't picture her youthful. She had little dimension and hardly any interests outside of temperamental mood swings, beating us, and snuff.

Her mother was a full-blooded Iroquois Indian named Mary Burns. Many Iroquois Indians were given the last name "Burns." Mary had married a European, John Champion.

There was something dark, mystical, and haunting about her heritage, paired with a meanness I couldn't fully comprehend. She was a woman who had never been properly loved, which hardened her, repelling people who might love her, which sadly led to a lack of love in her life.

Having grown up in a turbulent home, Mammy had always been a survivalist. It didn't help that she was half Native American. The late 1800s were cruel to darker skin tones and "half-breeds." Years later, when I was a teenager, Daddy told me that it was hard being a half-breed. They were outcast by both Europeans and Indians and usually poor. In an effort to escape her childhood (or perhaps in order to survive it), she began prostituting herself for all kinds of things: money, food, favors. This scenario was especially prevalent with peddlers that would come to the house selling goods: milk, fresh meat, special services.

This is how she became pregnant with all her children. She was old by the time she had Daddy, Emmitt Abner Champion, in 1889. She and her daughters were going by the last name of West. We assumed that the name had come from a new European husband her mother had married after her father John had died. So why she gave Daddy her own father's European last name, we'll never know. But Daddy's name was the most—and possibly the only—thoughtful thing Mammy had ever done. "Champion means he will overcome all struggles, and never be defeated by anything," she'd said. Essentially, she'd given birth to something greater than herself, that not even her most wicked demons could extinguish. My siblings and I believed the name itself must have protected Daddy from even the vilest experiences in Mammy's care.

After Mama died, Wayne and Daddy had gone to live with Mammy. Don and Brenda had stayed with relatives in Memphis. Once we all moved into Mammy's house, Wayne had cautioned me about her mood swings. He promised me that Daddy's visits on the weekend helped preserve the peace. Brenda and Don hadn't fully adjusted to Mammy's house either. They were too young to cope with the compounded trauma. They both stayed quiet most of the time.

Wayne mentioned always missing Daddy terribly when he had to go into town and stay there to work during the week. They'd bonded a lot while I'd been at Aunt Vertie's. Wayne learned the story about Daddy's limp that he'd protected us from our entire lives. Daddy said Wayne was finally old enough to know. It revealed a lot about Mammy.

In spite of himself, Wayne flinched as he retold the story of what really happened to Daddy's foot, and why he had a limp.

Mammy sent Daddy out to chop firewood when he was fourteen years old. Always mad about something, she kept screaming at him about how terrible of a job he was doing. Though Daddy's temper peaked, he rarely raised his voice back to Mammy.

Finally, she yelled, "You are not doing it right!" Which made Daddy lose his temper. He swung the ax as hard as he could, but missed, and chopped his foot on top, right around the ankle. He had cut through muscle, tendon, and bone. He collapsed.

There weren't many options for emergency healthcare back then, as you can imagine. And even if there were, he doubted Mammy would have considered it for a half second.

His foot was gushing blood and his adrenaline was wearing off, causing the pain to flood his entire body. With both his foot and his pride maimed, he laid on the ground lifeless, until he finally got the strength to get a needle and thread and sew his wound back together. His foot healed well enough to be functional, but the accident left an awful scar and a bad limp.

This was the final straw for Daddy after enduring more than a decade of abuse. Soon after that, he left home to begin a new life. He joined a lumberjack group and helped the cook until he was old enough to begin making a living in other ways. Daddy's limp hindered him for the rest of his life, professionally. But he never talked about it, because he preferred to look at the bright side, and choose hope.

Escaping Mammy and eventually finding Mama proved to Daddy that there was always a silver lining, always a promise of healing at the other side of a harrowing experience. Though I was beginning to understand why Aunt Maddie had been so determined to make him change his mind about us living with Mammy, I also suspected there was something greater in Daddy that wanted to forgive his mother. Right or wrong, he was setting out to give the best to his family and hoped that maybe his grace toward Mammy would create a change of heart in her. To his dismay, she proved to be the same dark spirit she had always been.

The first time Mammy hit me took me totally by surprise. I'd heard about her doing it to Daddy and his sisters, but I'd imagined, given my size and weight, that she might go easy on me. I'd been playing in the kitchen, humming—making some sort of sound she didn't like—and she slapped me. Knocked me right to the floor. No one had ever hit me with an open hand before, save the occasional blows I'd gotten accidentally from the cousins in games of tag. It made me mad more than it hurt me, and it certainly made me more cautious around her. But I was confident it wouldn't be the last time.

The slap flushed my face a bright pink but there was part of me that decided to contend with it. I'd persevered through Mama's death and Aunt Vertie's neglect. Like Daddy, I considered that we were all *just limping through life*. Every change of season and downturn was just another opportunity to do as we had been raised to do and cultivate hope.

While I didn't think my hope could redeem Mammy, I was confident it would help me learn how to deal with her. Little did I understand, this resolution would require much more than my six-year-old body had to offer. My soft, fragile bones already grieved Mama's death and the loss of our family's house. I was not ready for the trials Daddy had faced before me.

Chapter 11

The Shack

"The greater a child's terror, and the earlier it is experienced, the harder it becomes to develop a strong and healthy sense of self.
—Nathaniel Branden

Though we had little money, Mammy always had enough for snuff, which she kept in a tiny keepsake box. This made her nose and mouth smell, regardless of how she used it. We rarely came near her unpleasant face, but when she'd bellow, her thick, black breath would coat the air and permeate everything around her. If the snuff was packed away in her lip, it would sometimes show in the crevices of her mouth—making her appear all the more ghoulish. Her snuff habit made her seem harsh and masculine.

In the night, we'd hear her huff the thinly ground pieces up her nose. *Cough*. Then one more time for good measure. I wondered if it was the snuff that made her mean. Her use of it left a knot in the pit of my stomach. As she'd snort it, she'd sometimes hock and then spit. While I was always impressed when Wayne spit a far distance, I was disgusted at the sound, sight, and smell of Mammy's snuff in any form. Mammy was foul, and I would come to understand why no man had stayed around for very long—her edges were way too sharp.

Even after all the years of hardness, Daddy was always determined to keep things civil with Mammy. Especially as he relied on her to care for his babies. So, we crowded into her dilapidated shack in the woods with no front door. We were familiar with dirt and vermin. I was always surprised that a bear didn't walk right into the front room in the way birds and small rodents sometimes did. We were once afraid of these things, but we'd grown used to creatures scuttling around the shack throughout the night.

If a bear had wandered in, we'd have had little means of escape.

The house was made up of two rooms: a gross, old kitchen with a small space where we could sit in straight chairs, and a room with three beds. At night, Daddy and Wayne curled up in one bed. Mammy was in the other, which left Don, Brenda, and me in the smallest bed. During the summer, this was miserable. The stifling Mississippi heat was unforgiving. We'd wake up with sheets drenched in sweat and hair matted to our damp necks and foreheads. It was especially difficult when one of us would soil the bed. Daddy was careful to clean us up, but there was always the lingering threat that Mammy would beat us for it later.

Don had been potty-trained, but he reverted after Mama died. Aunt Dollie had tried to train him, but to no avail. Later in studies I learned some children do this as it is the only thing they have control of, but they really don't.

In the colder months, I was grateful to have warm bodies to curl up next to, my icy hands and feet would search for warmth beneath the thin covers.

Finding Don or Brenda's embrace on the other end made my skin hurt less as I drifted in and out of sleep.

At the end of the bed was a wooden chest. It was the most decorative thing Mammy owned and had a decent smell, despite everything in the shack absorbing body odor, the scent of tobacco, and sourness from the rain. Near our bed sat the only thing I owned, a little green chair, that was entirely mine from the old house. Of course, I had to share it. It was the only chair we children had. There were chairs at the kitchen table, but we mostly sat on the floor to eat.

The adjacent room was a dilapidated kitchen with a dish pan and a rust-covered wood-burning stove. At night mice would scuttle across it, scavenging for food, tucking crumbs away in their tiny jaws and gnawing as we tried to sleep. We also had little silverware; certainly not enough for all to sit down and have a full dinner. While we'd always been poor, I recognized this as a level of *without* that seemed strange to even me.

Now, we'd grown up in poverty, but didn't realize it. We didn't have much at all, but at least everything was clean, and there was an atmosphere of love and belonging. We were all we had, but we were all we needed, so we always had enough.

When you mix poverty with pure hatred, everything becomes a million times worse. The dilapidated structure of Mammy's house, the poorly kept grounds, the ragged furniture, and the outhouse in the back behind which all of us would all go squat to do our business, wiping with pages of Sears catalogs for toilet tissue—they all looked bleak and felt like hell on Earth.

Once, I asked Daddy why we had no money for what we needed, like soap, bacon, toilet paper, and running water. He said he was determined to pay what he owed to the hospital and the funeral home: for Mama's cancer treatment, for the coffin, and for the services. It was his character to ensure he rightfully pay every penny back. He was blindly loyal to the commemoration of Mama, and considered those payments his honor, due in part because he never could afford a headstone for her. He was tortured over this, and in turn kept himself in emotional pain over it, and unfortunately, this kept the rest of us in limbo in terms of our living situation and needs.

This settled a little when Wayne decided if we couldn't afford a proper tombstone for Mama, he would make one. None of us had much, but Wayne did have a toy hammer and chisel. So, he worked on it tirelessly. Every day. For weeks.

I begged him to let me help but he wouldn't, so I decided to find a rock of my own to memorialize Mama. I carefully chose mine. It was slate gray with a smooth surface and rounded edges. It looked softer than Wayne's, more feminine, from Mama's daughter. When Wayne was finally finished, we put the two-piece tombstone together in the yard and sat in front of it every day, talking to her as though she was right there with us.

Tombstone Wayne made for Mama

Wayne's workstation was a little wooden table in the yard that always shook beneath his project as he chiseled. He slaved away at his latest project, even when the days grew very hot. On a particularly sunny day, Don joined us at Wayne's table and watched him while he worked. The sun was shining on his face, illuminating his eyelashes, cheeks, and pink lips. His beautiful blue eyes sparkled in the streaming daylight. It felt like looking at a photograph. I studied him as though he was the most beautiful thing I had ever seen. Saying little, I put my hand out to him, and he held it.

But I winced when I saw that Don's toddler arms were covered with bruises as big as quarters. Mammy would beat him every chance she got, usually for small things that were beyond his control. We noticed that Mammy was especially weird about bowel movements. Private parts triggered her. She punished all her children for having them. Don was barely potty trained again.

In the winter and in bad weather, we did have a potty. It was called a *slop jar.* It was thick with feces and rarely cleaned. I'd hold my nose when I'd use it, and gag when the smell became too much. When little

Don used the slop jar, he had a hard time managing his little boy body parts, so Mammy would hit him. She'd hit him for aiming and missing. She'd hit him for making a mess *outside*. She'd hit him when he'd hold his urine out of fear, then wet himself. She'd hit him *just because*. She hit me that way, too. Brenda, still basically an infant, was mercilessly left alone most of the time, although being ignored as a baby is another kind of abuse altogether. Thankfully, Mammy never hit Wayne.

I was accustomed to being slapped off the slop pot when my bowel movements were *too loud*. When I pulled my skirt up too high while trying to figure out *how to not* get my clothing and feet wet. And when trying to wipe myself exposed too much of my body. Blunt force trauma in the most private, intimate spaces was Mammy's specialty. She derived a great sense of control when we couldn't escape her. And although I am certain Daddy couldn't have been blind to all the bruises that covered his children's bodies, he was very aware that if he confronted her and she threw him out, he'd lose us all. There was only so much that could be done.

Eyeing Don's fragile, black-and-blue baby skin made my soul ache. I pulled him into me and whispered, "I will never let her hurt you again, I promise."

That day, we found three spots together that would be his outdoor *hiding places* when Mammy's mood took a downturn. One was behind the chicken house, one was behind the shack, and one was in a thicket of bushes out in the woods. We made a pact that if I ever noticed her reeling, I would give him the sign. "Run," I'd mouth or whisper. Then he'd dart out the door and wait in the dense brush until I could come for him.

From that day forward, it was common for me to use my soft, six-year-old body as a shield between Mammy and Don. I'd stand, arms out and flailing, willing to take as many hits as I needed while he ran and hid. I'd picture him darting out of the house and being safe. The house was at the very bottom of a high hill. I could hear people at the top of the hill in houses and yards, wondering why they couldn't hear or help us. Especially because Mammy's rants were either sharp, loud, and quick, or beatings that would last forever, until our tiny, weeping, child bodies collapsed. The louder we were, the angrier she'd become. Our shrieks would echo throughout the valley surrounding the shack. Noise carried up the hill —and still no one came for us.

Mammy's favorite mind game was to attempt to get Wayne and me to admit to things we hadn't done (and would never do). Luckily, I'd inherited one trait from her that would protect me from her scheming: stubbornness. While I'll never know for sure if being stubborn saved my life, I know it helped me stave off Mammy's evil. I've often wondered if on some subconscious level she even respected me for it.

She'd come at me full force with a list of accusations, telling me to forfeit the fight . . . *admit I did it!* But I would never concede. The more I would say I didn't do it, the more angry she would become. I knew if I gave in to her, even once, she would never stop. So, I never bent to her will. Especially if I knew Daddy would be back soon.

Mammy left marks all over me, but because we played outside so much, they could be passed off as childhood scrapes, so she always had an alibi. We'd be healed up enough by the time Daddy returned from his week at work, so we found it pointless and hopeless to tell Daddy. Though Mammy had a history of violent behavior, we didn't know the full extent of their relationship and were worried he wouldn't believe us. And worse, we worried, *What if we couldn't escape her after we told?*

It wasn't worth the risk. So, we were obedient to Mammy, and complied with her threats when it made sense, namely with chores. I would do my chores with diligence because it made Daddy happy. Plus, I promised Mama before she died I would take care of things in the way she'd taught me.

One of my favorite jobs was going to the creek to get water, because we didn't have a well. It was heavy for my small hands. But when I carried it, I loved knocking it along fence posts and rocks to hear the different sounds I could make. I especially loved singing into it.

The walk was scenic in the warmer months. Birds would tuck themselves away in the leafy green trees and whistle as I walked down to the creek. Usually, the water was freezing even in the summer months, but I enjoyed running my hands through it. I still love water, and the way the light hits its surface at different times of the day. I grew accustomed to the creek because I made several trips there a day. I made the first trip as soon as I woke up. When Daddy was home, he'd join me, and we would have *the best* time.

I loved long walks with Daddy, even if we said nothing. He was gone so much I'd get nervous butterflies during our alone time, like the way you feel when you are first getting to know someone all over again.

Daddy had changed without Mama. He looked tired, weathered, and sunken in. But I'd slip my tiny hand into his and see his big, broad smile widen the way it used to. When we'd walk together to get water, he'd carry the large, clunky bucket. He would fill the bucket full to save me a trip. I could only carry it half full.

One spring day, we made it down to the creek bed and I took my shoes off. I sunk my bare feet into the wet soil as Daddy bent over to scoop up the cool, crystalline water with our pail. Suddenly, I felt a strange sensation and looked down to see a long snake slivering over my toes. I let out a blood-curdling shriek that made Daddy jump up in fear and drop the water bucket.

"Stop, Gail! Stop screaming!" he yelled, telling me the snake would be scared of me and would go away on its own. As I breathed, eyes wide, I watched the long, slick creature slink away and dip beneath a mound of rocks. Daddy comforted me, wrapped me up, and held me until my heartbeat slowed. I breathed in his smell for the first time in what felt like ages. It felt like our whole family was wrapped up in one big hug. I stayed there, holding onto a sense of safety, feeling grateful to experience *home*. This kept me feeling safe at the creek, even when Daddy wasn't there with me.

My incident with the snake made me even better at hide-and-seek. I didn't fear creepy crawling things as much as my siblings. They couldn't hold it together (especially Brenda) if they felt something brush past them. They'd make a noise and then I'd find them! *Tag! You're it!* I'd scream, then chase each other all the way back to the house.

There were no rules when we'd play hide-and-seek. Anywhere outside or inside was fair game. During one game, I made my way back up to the house to throw Don off. Being younger than me, he'd get lost in counting and I'd have the advantage. I ran until my heart was pounding in my ears and my cheeks were flushed. My raggedy sundress flapped in the wind. I wasn't mindful about keeping it pulled down.

After bounding over the threshold of the shack, I dove under a bed, thinking the quiet, dark space would be the perfect place to conceal my small body. I was quiet, knowing Mammy was in the kitchen preparing something on the stove that smelled like it was burning. On my belly, I scooted forward, pulling myself along with my upper body strength.

My siblings rushed in behind me and I held my breath, hoping to be practically invisible. I tucked my fist under my racing heart as I watched Don and Brenda's feet scuttle past and then out.

Out abruptly.

Out with big, bounding feet behind them.

Mammy's feet moved aggressively with every step. My body stiffened at the sight of them.

Surely, she won't find me, I thought.

And then—shrieks!

My own shrieks.

And blinding, scalding pain.

I wasn't sure what had happened at first. I only felt searing heat on my exposed legs, up to my thighs. As I writhed in agony, Mammy grabbed my bare foot and pulled me out from under the bed into the daylit room. In one hand, she held a pot. She towered over me with one fist raised, and a wild look on her face. She'd seen my panties and my small bare legs under the bed and had chosen to make an example of me by tossing a pot of hot water under the bed, dousing my private parts.

I shrieked and cried. Then rage eclipsed my pain and I jumped up to my feet so angry at her, I wanted to attack. I wanted to primitively claw at her skin and hair and snuff-stained mouth. But when I hurled my body forward to fight, I found my legs doing the opposite of what I had intended: I was not running *toward* Mammy, I was running away from her.

With all my adrenaline and all my might, my body took over to defend itself. My legs and private parts were burning with a burn that wouldn't stop. I was reassured to know my legs worked just fine. I let them carry me *away*.

Later, Wayne got some old rags, put them in the water bucket, and put them on me.

Chapter 12

Champion

"Be strong and courageous. Do not be afraid or terrified because of them, for the LORD your God goes with you; he will never leave you nor forsake you."
—Deuteronomy 31:6

Daddy had always loved music. Our pleasant memories at Mammy's house consisted of getting into the back seat of his car to listen to the radio. Just like when Mama was alive. Every now and then he'd cast his worries about money aside and take all of us children to the store to get a cold drink and candy bar. The drinks were a full nickel. Nehi Grape soda had the thickest, syrupiest feeling on my tongue, and the yummiest taste in the world. Wayne said it *tasted* purple, and he was right! I always wanted to make mine last by bringing it with me and sipping it slowly, but we had to drink them in the store, because Daddy got three cents back for every glass bottle he returned.

When we were all together, it reminded me of old times. Except now we all had years and pain on us. We were different. The way we laughed together was more melancholic, almost as if we were guests around each other.

As a child, I often wondered if Daddy had *ever* speculated Mammy was abusing us. But as I grew to become a mother and grandmother myself, *I know that he knew*. And I'm sure it tore him apart that he didn't have any other options than to let his children, whom he loved dearly, be abused by the woman who had abused him and his siblings so badly.

He wasn't often able to afford extra gifts for us. But one holiday, Daddy did the most marvelous thing while we lived with Mammy. On Friday night, he came home somewhat lighthearted, smiling a little broader than usual. I felt like something special was about to happen.

When he pulled a big bag of something out of the car, Wayne knew right away and said, "Fireworks!"

I didn't know what that meant but I found out when it got dark. There were Roman Candles, sparklers, and even firecrackers. The smell was wonderful. The colors were the most amazing thing I had ever seen. Daddy made sure we stood far enough away to be safe. Wayne helped him.

I'll never forget the first time I held a sparkler in my hand, in awe of the bright light as it sent flashes into the dark. I was excited all night and sad it was over all at the same time.

Another time, during the winter, there was talk of Christmas, especially by Wayne. He had to explain what Christmas and Santa Claus were. It seemed like something exciting.

Daddy was coming home for the week, but it wasn't Christmas yet. He brought each of us a most wonderful gift, a tiny snow globe. (I'm sure the globes were cheap or even free with a purchase of some kind). We all liked them, but as usual, I was more fascinated than the rest. I thought it was wonderful. Wayne had seen them before. Don and Brenda were too little to appreciate them.

I remember every detail of mine. There was a tiny house, a couple of tiny trees, a very tiny dog, and people.

I sat on the only step going into Mammy's house. I would shake the snow globe, let it settle and shake it again . . . over and over. The water reminded me of Steenson Hollow. We had already seen snow that winter.

When the soft snow would fall on the tiny people in the globe, it didn't seem cold. I wondered if it was warm in the house because there was a tiny puff of smoke connected to the chimney. I knew the people had to be happy.

I began to imagine me being in there with them, and also the rest of us. The more I played with it, the more I dreamed I could get in there somehow. I kept it for a long time but I don't remember what became of it. It was a wonderful gift Daddy gave us all.

One Friday, I was running outside with Don and our screaming during a game of tag had gotten too loud. Out of nowhere, Mammy blocked my route and clotheslined me with her arm, then proceeded to beat me with a *switch* she'd snapped off a tree. She grabbed and pinched my left arm as hard as she could to keep me from getting away. So I laid back on the ground and began kicking my legs at her. This made her fly into a blind rage. She started swatting me with the thin, prickly stick as hard as possible on my bare arms, legs, and neck. She wore herself out beating me. Usually I tried to keep my wails down, but I shrieked the whole time, hoping to draw attention to what was happening, hoping a grown-up on the hilltop would at least come outside to see what the commotion was. I could see the roofs of their houses. I'm sure they heard, but no one came.

The next day, when Daddy got home, I was still sore. He noticed that I was covered in bruises. He asked what I'd done. Mammy interjected, saying I was running outside and fell. I didn't have the stamina to disagree with her.

Mammy made everything impossible. No one was allowed to be content around her, and certainly not excited. Because everyone had little money, I rarely got gifts. But Aunt Gladys treated me once, for no reason at all, to the *most beautiful dress* I had ever seen. Well, I thought it was a dress—it was a silk slip with a tiny bow at the top. Aunt Gladys insisted it belonged *under* a dress—I couldn't wear it on its own. But I couldn't understand why, so I just put it on. I was amazed at its whiteness, the delicate pink flowers, and little ribbon bow at the bottom that looked like a "V."

Given Mammy's hatred of body parts, she saw me in the slip and insisted I take it off. She said she was going to put it *away* in the wooden chest. I knew this meant I would never see the slip again. Wanting to steal a few more moments of something glorious, I refused to take it off. So, she grabbed a stick. She had one in both rooms of the house.

My whole body tensed. I knew she was about to really hurt me. My siblings were incredibly scared. I'm not entirely sure how I got the courage, but my body shot away from her. I jumped on Daddy's bed before she could grab me. I crawled across it as she reached for me, and gathered myself up into a tiny ball between the bed and the wall.

My body was just small enough to fit. I knew she could not fit in that tiny space. So, I stayed on the floor for what felt like forever. She was out of my sight, and I thought if I couldn't see her, then she couldn't see me.

Thinking I'd outwitted her, I peeked over the top of the bed. She was back in the kitchen.

It was odd. I'd never seen her give up before. This new response made me even more afraid. My body began trembling, fearing punishment by hot water again. Or maybe she was thinking of an evil I'd never experienced before, something I couldn't even imagine.

Having lost the joy of the moment, I took the slip off, exposing a tiny body covered in injuries from the last beating. I put on an outfit that draped over every inch of me, then carefully folded my gift and quietly placed it on the wooden chest as a truce. I knew that that was the last of my fun, and the slip would disappear with the few other gifts my siblings and I had ever received. I was grateful that for a moment I got to experience something beautiful, before I had to forfeit it entirely.

I have only one memory of Mammy doing well by me. She saved my life once.

We had been discouraged from going into the backyard. Mammy hated it back there. It was a brush-covered mess, full of thorns, sticks, and wily plants. The odds of being bitten by an insect or snake were high, so we steered clear.

One day, Wayne and I decided we were bored with the front yard. We went around back. There, we found a large hole in the wood of the house at eye level. In the back was a perfectly crafted wasp's nest. I stared at it, not knowing what it was. I called Wayne over to see it. I put my hand on it to bring it out for him. He didn't know what I was doing, or he would have stopped me. Within seconds, my fascination broke: I was being stung so violently my whole body heated up. I ran screaming but I couldn't escape the tiny, angry, red insects that seemed to be trailing me. I was stung so many times I passed out.

When I awoke the next morning, I was lying on a quilt on the floor. A big dog, which I had never seen before, was licking me. I was too weak to be frightened. Wayne was hovering over me, making sure I was okay. He told me Mammy had borrowed the dog from the neighbor man to help lick the venom out.

I slipped in and out of consciousness. Every time I awoke, the dog was there. Sometimes licking me. Sometimes not. The dog and the neighbor's kindness had saved my life. Evidently, he'd come from the big white house near the woods. It was the nicest house for miles. When Daddy met the neighbor to return the dog, he shook the man's hand and gave them his name.

"Champion?" The man said. "Well! I wonder if we're related. That's my last name, too."

"No sir," Daddy said kindly, "I don't believe I've ever had a relative that had money. But I'm happy to share a name with anyone so kind."

I was grateful the dog had saved my life, to a degree. The stings, along with the mounting wounds inflicted by Mammy were beginning to be more than my tiny body could endure. I assumed I had to be reaching some kind of threshold.

Nothing will hurt more than the wasp stings, I told myself as I slowly regained my strength over the next few days. *Nothing.*

But I was very wrong.

Chapter 13

Kill Me, I Don't Care

"Sometimes even to live is an act of courage."
—Lucius Annaeus Seneca

It was Monday. Daddy had gone to work for the week. He would return on Friday to spend the weekend at home with us. Mammy was inside as I watched Daddy drive off. After seeing him off, I started making my way out to the chicken house to use the bathroom. Mammy had, at some point, stepped in front of me and was also walking to the same spot. Our bodies neared each other just enough to where I could have reached out and touched her, when suddenly, her foot caught on a root sticking out of the ground, and she fell.

I stood there, shocked. I'd never seen her in a position of vulnerability. She shook her head, dizzy with confusion, and then her eyes went black. Whether she thought I tripped her, or just needed to take her frustration out on someone, I'll never know.

She said, "You pushed me down!" But I knew I hadn't. She quickly stood, grabbed my arm, and dragged me toward the shack until we were in the front room. She picked up her ever-ready switch and began to beat me, over, and over, and over again.

I'd seen her mad before, but I'd never seen her crazed. It was as if a wild animal had been provoked and had broken out of its cage. She hit to harm, possibly to kill.

"You are bad!" she yelled.

"I am not!" I screamed back, wincing, and holding out my arms to protect my body.

"Say you are bad!" she demanded.

"I will not!" I held my ground. I wouldn't give in that easily. Daddy had always said I was the best little girl in the whole world. I knew if I said I was *bad* it would somehow make Daddy wrong. I just couldn't do that.

She continued yelling, "Say it! Say, *'I am bad!'*"

I shut my mouth tight, keeping all my words in. Then, she began hitting my face with the stick, a place she'd never struck with a switch before. She hoisted up my little green chair and hit me on my back with one of the legs. A little chip broke off and flew through the air. For an instant, I forgot everything that was happening and watched the chip soar in what felt like slow motion. I was in total amazement that the color of the material on the inside was different from the color on the outside.

Then she grabbed a bigger chair as she thrust me to the floor again. She put the chair over my body and sat in it, pinning me down as she beat me. I could hardly see. I knew the others were outside, horrified. So, I started telling myself it was okay to just lay there. *It's okay to die.* I told myself. *There's a better place than this.*

"Go ahead and kill me," I yelled with my last remaining conscious breath, "I'll go be with Mama."

Suddenly, other voices rang out. It was the sound of my siblings shouting, "Daddy, Daddy!" But Daddy was at work for the week. I didn't know why they were calling for him. Then, just like that, in the doorway, there he was.

In a flash, he lunged at Mammy and threw her across the room. She landed on a bed. Then he picked up the chair and threw it across the room against the wall. He gathered me up and rushed me to the hospital, but I don't remember the ride or anything else until I awoke days later.

As I regained consciousness, I heard voices unfamiliar to me. I assumed I'd died and was in Heaven. I wondered where Mama was. I saw angels all in white. They were walking around me, touching me with something cool. It felt good but I was also aware of pain . . . everywhere. And Daddy was there.

"Are you dead too?" I asked him. He shook his head *no,* as he began to cry. This told me we were very much alive because people didn't cry in Heaven. Then I realized how badly my back hurt. I already knew that the healing from being beaten always hurt worse than the beating itself.

I would later learn the very sad reason Daddy inexplicably came back home on Monday. One of his coworkers had committed suicide by standing in front of the train Daddy was driving. At that time, Daddy was a train conductor for Reynolds Aluminum. He conducted each train's movement from inside a building, not from inside the individual train. The trains only went around the plant to move things from one place to another.

For some unknown reason, one of his coworkers had picked that day to be his last and chose that specific time. When the train was moving on the tracks, the man stood on the tracks in front of it. I imagine the man had to have been thinking about doing it for a while, since that's an awful way to die. So, they sent Daddy home because they had to investigate the death.

I can't imagine the mental anguish Daddy must have felt, coming home early, shaken from knowing a coworker died, maybe aided by his hands. And then to come home to the horror of finding your own mother trying to murder your precious child.

A few weeks later, an X-ray showed that my rib had been broken. I would have to suffer through its healing, and not be able to see Mama after all. I was disappointed.

On one occasion while I was in the hospital recovering, strangers in nice clothes stood all around me. They looked fancy. I didn't know why they were in my room. Then one day not long after, a man brought me a dress and shoes and took me with him to his car. Thankfully, I was no longer hurting so badly. We may have talked during the drive, but he didn't have much to say. Gradually, the roads became familiar to me, and I realized we were going back to Mammy's house. My stomach filled with dread.

When we got there, the whole family was standing in the front yard. We got out, and Daddy wrapped me up in a hug and wept. The feeling of heaviness was thick around us. Even Mammy was sad.

"I'm sorry," Mammy said. "I don't know why I did it." She reached for me, but I didn't want her to touch me. I clung to Daddy's neck.

After what felt like the longest hour, Daddy and Wayne got into Daddy's car and drove off. Then the same man that picked me up from the hospital drove me, Brenda, and Don to a nearby park. Daddy and Wayne were there waiting for us. I saw food spread out. We were going to have a family picnic! I thought of the last family picnic we'd had together by the lake, and how time stood still as I watched Mama cuddle Don and Brenda by the big tree. Before everything changed.

I wouldn't learn until years later that after Mammy tried to kill me, while I was still in the hospital, Daddy had to appear before the juvenile judge, a kind man by the name of Zimmerman. He let Daddy tell the whole story. He must have felt such an awful weight, but he knew he had to truly do right by us children.

"You cannot keep all of your children," he told Daddy. "You cannot afford them. You don't have anybody to help you. You can keep the three, or you can keep the one, but you can't keep them all." By "the one" he meant Wayne.

Judge Zimmerman gave Daddy a few days to look for places where Wayne could go, but he never found a place that was equipped to take care of his physical needs, where people would also love him just like any other normal child. Daddy knew the three of us younger children would be loved and taken care of in a court-appointed foster home, but Wayne would not be, because there were so few people who could care for special needs children. He would not let Wayne go.

Toward the end of our picnic, I started to get that feeling in my stomach again. I knew something wasn't right. Why was this strange man still standing next to his car watching us have a picnic? Before Daddy could get the words out of his mouth, I knew we were leaving him again.

After we'd finished our meals, the man walked over and told all of us to sit next to each other at the picnic table for a family picture. Wayne was to the left of Daddy and I was on the right, with Don and Brenda between his knees. None of us children looked happy. In fact, Brenda is downright scowling at the man behind the camera. Daddy tried to give his best smile for the camera but when I look at the picture now, I clearly see the years of pain, and the disappointment that life hadn't at all turned out the way Daddy dreamed it would when he married Mama.

Daddy hugged Don, Brenda, and me one last time. This is what loss felt like. I knew it as well as I knew the sound of each of my sibling's breath. Then we got back into the car with the man and drove away, watching Daddy and Wayne shrink into smaller versions of themselves until we couldn't see them anymore. I don't know if any of us cried. We were probably too bone-tired to show any emotion at all.

Sometime later, we arrived at another house. The man opened the door and helped me get out, but Brenda and Don stayed in the car. I later learned the man who came to pick us up was from the Welfare Department. We were being ushered into government care. I wasn't sure what that meant, but I figured it had to be a better place than the shack.

Chapter 14

Foster Care

"Fear not, for I am with you; be not dismayed, for I am your God; I will strengthen you, I will help you, I will uphold you with my righteous right hand."
—Isaiah 41:10

Mr. and Mrs. Smith were the caretakers at my first foster home. They seemed like a nice couple. They and their daughter liked me and were very kind. Debbie was a little older than me so I got beautiful clothes and shoes she had outgrown. I perceived that they enjoyed hosting foster children. I felt secure in their home. It was a nice place to recover. Since it was the summer months, we didn't go to school.

Though my first foster home had been safe, I'd hardly adjusted before my caretaker Mrs. Smith was diagnosed with cancer. The news made my heart sick and my stomach weak. I knew what cancer had done to Mama. I later learned she survived. When I was in my late teens, Mr. and Mrs. Smith and Debbie came to see me.

The same man came to take me to another house. I was happy because the government had done their best to keep Don, Brenda, and me physically close to each other.

Brenda and Don were living with the Butlers. They only had room for two foster children. They talked their next-door neighbors the Halls, into becoming foster parents so they could take me.

We only had a long driveway separating us. I was able to see them as much as I wanted. Our shared sense of relief—having escaped evil Mammy—freed all of us.

We adapted to the hot, sticky summer months, filled with flourishing blossom trees and my favorite fleecy clouds. We talked of going to school in September. We spent our days eating popsicles that would melt too quickly, running barefoot through our new, plush, backyards, and separating when the twilight came to usher us off to our soft, safe beds.

I wondered about Wayne. I was sad he'd been forced to stay behind with Daddy and wretched Mammy. I hated that his unique needs always kept us separated. I wished I could have talked to him and told him that we were all safe and that he didn't have to worry, to ease some of the burden of us being raised apart.

Don, Brenda, and I ached for Daddy. But due to his work schedule he wasn't able to visit us but once. When he did, it was such a special occasion. Mrs. Butler took us to a nearby park. It was one of the hottest days of the year, but we didn't care.

When Daddy pulled up in the parking lot with Wayne in the car, we jumped, screamed, and raced toward his car. After helping Wayne out of the passenger seat, Daddy opened the trunk and pulled out a box. We gathered around to see the delicious foods he'd packed: baloney, fruit, and bottles of Nehi grape. He even brought chips and chocolate, which we rarely got to eat. We were thrilled.

We played all day on every piece of equipment. Daddy pushed us in the swings, caught us on the slide, and helped us cross the monkey bars. He even joined us in an evening game of hide-and-seek as the sun began to sink below the lavender horizon. The excitement in the air became all the more glorious as Daddy began hugging us individually. He held us for a long time and affirmed his love for us. Then, we must have joined in a group hug for five whole minutes before the mutual feeling of celebration began to transition into melancholy. While the embraces overwhelmed us with tremendous joy, they inevitably meant something sad.

Daddy and Wayne were leaving soon—and as always, we didn't know when we would see them again.

When the woman from the Welfare Department came to take us back to our respective homes, Daddy wrapped me up a final time saying, "Be good, Gail. Promise me."

"I will Daddy," I responded through tears. I deeply inhaled his scent, so I could memorize it before I left.

Then he helped Wayne into his car. Don, Brenda, and I climbed into the other as our paths, once again, parted ways.

Back then, it was very common for people to take their children to a matinee and leave them there, sometimes for hours. Mrs. Hall would take her daughter and me to the movies. She even gave her daughter money to buy us both a snack. I didn't know much about candy bars. I'd only had a few in my entire life since they cost money we often didn't have, but I knew I wanted one.

Instead, the daughter bought me a box of pretzels. I remember her saying, "Everybody is eating these."

I thought, *I'm somebody and I'm not eating them*. I didn't like them at all. I wanted a candy bar so badly.

The second time we went to the movies, the daughter bought me a box of pretzels again and I didn't even open them. I placed the box on the floor next to my seat. The next time we headed for the movies, I said to her mother, "Don't give her money for my pretzels because I don't like pretzels."

"What do you mean?" She asked.

I said, “We get pretzels every week and I don’t like them.”

“What do you want?”

I said, “A candy bar.”

She told her daughter, “From now on, let her get what she wants.”

The next time we went to the movies, I got the candy bar that looked the biggest. The Baby Ruth candy bars were pretty big back then. It’s the first time I remember deliberately speaking up and getting my way. I had made up my mind beforehand. I could get what I wanted. I didn’t have to get that box of pretzels every week and put them on the floor for somebody to throw away.

It was such a wonderful feeling that day. I felt triumphant, even if it was only a candy bar. It was the first time I had felt that way in a very long time, like I could figure out how to get what I wanted and then do it.

Chapter 15

Childhaven

"For I know the plans I have for you," declares the LORD, "plans to prosper you and not to harm you, plans to give you hope and a future."
—Jeremiah 29:11

One day, Mrs. Hall walked me over to the Butlers' house again. Brenda and Don were already on the sofa, sitting near a woman I would come to know as Mother Lee. I sat by her husband, who was called Daddy Brock. He wore a navy suit with a yellow-and-white-striped tie. He was a handsome man, though almost bald. He put an arm around me and thanked me for sitting with him. I fell in love with them that day.

This lovely couple introduced themselves and began talking to us about going to live somewhere else. Though I wasn't sure what they were talking about, I sensed it was somewhere safe. My heart and mind were bathed in a warm, comforting sensation, like the way I used to feel when Mama would hold me. As I studied their beautiful faces, I wondered if Mama was watching all of us from her place among the white, fluffy clouds in the sky that day. Whether it was Mama, the angels, or God, I sensed *something* good was ahead.

The only thing I really understood was that we were going to live with them—a wonderful thought. But not now. "But when?" I asked. Someone would come for us in a few days and take us to them.

"How did you find us?" I asked.

Mother Lee beamed at this question, as if she couldn't wait to tell the story of my rescue. Daddy Brock listened, hanging on every word she said, as though he was hearing it for the first time.

"When you were in the hospital, your daddy was very worried about you. He went before a judge to find a safe place for you all to go. A place that is warm, safe, and lovely," she said. "We have something special in mind for you soon. There's a wonderful, big house with a long white fence surrounded by fields full of grass and wildflowers as far as the eye can see. It's a place children go when they need to feel safe. There is yummy food, bedtime stories, and lots of playing. We would like you to come stay with us. Do you think you would like that?" Mother Lee asked.

As it turned out, Daddy asked Judge Zimmerman to put us in the care of members of Churches of Christ, as he was a member. Judge Zimmerman knew some Christians had recently bought Childhaven. This is why we ended up going there after foster care.

My heart was soothed at the sound of Childhaven. I trusted Mother Lee and Daddy Brock. The picture she'd painted sounded wonderful, it brought me peace just thinking about it.

A nice man and woman from the Welfare Department came and picked us up one day and took us to the park. Wayne and Daddy were already there. Brenda wanted to play instead of getting her picture made. So, in one of the two photos made that day, she has a snarl on her face. In the other, she is trying to run off. Wayne is dragging her back by the tail of her dress.

Wayne, Don, Daddy, Brenda, and I on the day we went to Childhaven

After the picnic, we said goodbye to Daddy and Wayne all over again. I knew we were going somewhere else. Although I don't remember bringing anything with us. The man and woman from the Welfare Department said all we needed would be given to us when we got there.

"Go where?" I asked.

A place called Childhaven.

It was a long way to Cullman, Alabama. More hours than I could count as I nodded off and woke up to a new strip of scenery.

"You'll know we're almost there when you see the long, white fence," the lady driving said to us.

When it finally came into view and the car slowed, I was bursting with anticipation and sat up on my knees next to Don and Brenda, rolling down the window to see the full picture. In the distance was the biggest house I'd ever seen—a white, sparkling, plantation home that seemed to melt into the sky. The outside was landscaped with perfectly sculpted shrubs, vibrant yellow mums, and lots of crepe myrtles. I could hardly believe this place was for me—for us.

On the large porch there were two children taking turns with a jump rope, and next to them were friendly caretakers, rocking back and forth in rockers. The magnitude of the place was unlike anything I'd ever seen.

When we finally parked, I was trembling with excitement. I followed slowly behind the lady, captivated by my surroundings. When we reached the sprawling stone front steps, she extended her hand and asked warmly, "Are you ready to see your new home?"

I cried from joy. I was surprised to feel big, wet, happy tears streaming down my face.

I nodded, and a man opened the door, saying, "Ladies first!"

And we stepped over the threshold into my brand-new life.

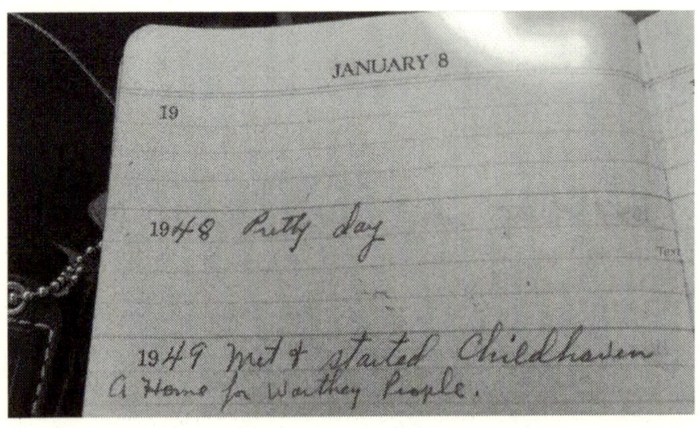

JANUARY 8

19

1948 Pretty day

1949 Met & started Childhaven A Home for Worthey People.

From the diary of Pop Myers, a member of the original 1949 Childhaven board:
"January 8, 1949: Met & started Childhaven. A Home for Worthy People."

Childhaven, a home for children, had begun as a wonderful idea on January 8, 1949, and came to fruition in 1951 when it opened. Four children in the King family were the first residents. Sherry, just over two years old, was the baby. The other siblings were Mildred, Tommy, and Wade. Their eldest sister Hilda was in the hospital having surgery on her eyes at that time. In 1951, Brenda, Don, and I became children numbers five, six, and seven.

When I arrived at Childhaven at the age of eight, I was the oldest child there. Childhaven would be the setting for the latter half of my childhood and teenage years. Within months of our arrival, there were many more children.

The house was broken up into apartments: each had four rooms and a room for the houseparent assigned to that space, as well as a bathroom and laundry room. All the houseparents had a lovely temperament except one who could be a little dislikable at times. They were intentional about building relationships with all of us—even if they weren't our primary caretakers. In the early years, the houseparents were single women except Daddy Pie and Mother Sparkie who kept the nursery.

Mother Lee invited us into the grand entry hall. It had high ceilings, and a wide cylinder cut in the ceiling that extended for five floors, with a glass dome at the top for light, and windows around each floor. The staircase with a banister went up into long hallways full of magnificent rooms which would become bedrooms. The rooms were not ready for children yet but would be in about a month when other children started coming.

The nursery was one big room on the main floor. It had previously been an auditorium. Today it is where Childhaven board meetings take place. There was an Executive Directors Office and a beautiful area to entertain visitors.

Beds were side by side against two walls. On the other wall were sinks and shelves. There was a stage to play on and closets where clothes were kept. In the entry hall there was a room for houseparents, and bathrooms on the other side.

The nursery was set up for children under the age of five. I was eight when I was taken to Childhaven, which meant I would receive my own bed in the nursery for just a short period of time while the upper floor was being restored.

I was swept away in what felt like a dream. This made me feel simultaneously happy and sad. I didn't want to forget Daddy. I was worried the less time I spent focusing on memories of him the more he would fade in my mind, the way Mama had. So, I was committed to making myself remember, so that I could keep the best parts of my old life with me.

After touring the nursery and the children's bathroom, Mother Lee walked us through the rest of the house, including the sitting room, the whole time reciting interesting facts about the property, its original owners, and the history of the land that wove into the culture of Cullman, Alabama.

The house had been built back in the 1800s by the Odd Fellows, a group very similar to the Freemasons. That was, until the Tennessee Valley Authority bought it from them and adapted the house to be its headquarters. For years they only used a portion of the house, as it was far too big for practical business. In time, they decided that serving the community would put this magnificent house with all its unique amenities to better use.

Odd Fellows Home (Childhaven), image from Cullman County Museum

Though it all seemed too beautiful to touch, it belonged to all of us. We were fully allowed and encouraged to explore as much as our hearts desired.

After showing us the dining room, Mother Lee and Daddy Brock took us into their apartment. The door swung open to a cozy scene: a spruce green couch with clawed feet covered by a stack of cozy looking quilts, and a matching decorative chair with elaborate wooden arms. On the coffee table there were children's books. The seating area faced a fireplace with a mantle decorated with fresh flowers and photographs of the family. There was also big framed pictures of both of their children.

From the back hallway emerged a child. It was their son, Del. He was around twelve years old and very kind. He welcomed us *home* by inviting us to play with him sometime. I gave him a hearty *yes*. Mother Lee was pleased to see that I was already adapting well.

Mother Lee and Daddy (Barney) Brock

We were then shown their daughter Wrenda's room. She was a tiny little thing with curly blond ringlets. When we entered, we immediately quieted, as she was lying face down with her hands beside her, fully asleep. The sight of her there looked like something I'd only seen in picture books at school. A tiny girl, wearing a plaid, yellow dress, peacefully sleeping on her cozy bed. All that was missing was a little black dog beside her. I was amazed that any child could resemble a doll so well.

All the children were well-behaved and very kind. We had a mutual understanding that life prior to this had been *difficult*. As a result, we shared a mutual awe and appreciation of Mother Lee and Daddy Brock, not to mention the fascinating houseparents that all seemed to have distinct personalities.

There were Daddy Pie and Mother Sparkie. I never did learn their real names, but I found out that *Pie* and *Sparkie* were nicknames they'd gone by in the community long before they'd come to Childhaven. While the *moms* and the *dads* of the house took care of the children, Sparkie's sister Rean's specialty was cooking. She loved preparing meals for the family. Rean made sure no one ever went hungry. There was a space at the table for everyone.

Outside the house, Fred the groundskeeper oversaw the landscaping, mowing, and repairs. Though he kept to himself, he'd always look up from his work to give a nod and a friendly wave. We respected his efforts by staying out of the flower beds. We were appreciative when he'd come late at night to fix the plumbing in the bathroom or bring in coal for the furnace to warm us up during the colder months.

In many ways the first seven children were like the seven dwarves. During the day we played and explored our new surroundings. At night, we nestled in our beds as Mother Lee or Daddy Brock would come in to read us a bedtime or Bible story. We always kept the nightlight on for the little ones who were afraid of the dark. If one of the babies had nightmares, the older children would curl up with them to make them feel safe. We fell in love with the place early on. We deeply enjoyed each other's company, especially playing outdoors.

On one portion of the land there was a large playground, complete with a massive swing set, metal slide, and a brightly painted merry-go-round. It was hard to top the wonder of Childhaven. So, most of our playtime took place in the comfort of our own home.

We'd been traveling all day and though the lady had brought us snacks for the road, the wafting smells of fresh cornbread and slow-cooking chili made my mouth water. But I'd been so tired after the tour with Mother Lee, that I had fallen asleep next to her on the downstairs sofa. She stayed beside me, reading her book, throughout the early evening, so that I wouldn't feel alone when I awoke. By 7 p.m. my eyes flickered open to see nightfall outside the window.

Mother Lee nudged me and warmly said, "It's time to eat dinner!" She got up and invited me to follow her. She led me past the dining room into the massive kitchen. All the other children had eaten already, but Mother Lee had let me sleep, figuring I'd be better off resting.

In the kitchen she scooped up a delicious bowl of chili for me, with melted cheese on top. It was the tastiest thing I'd ever eaten. Every scoop made my stomach feel full, and my heart feel more at home. As I heaped one huge spoonful into my mouth after another (sometimes dropping small bits on my shirt), I glanced up at Mother Lee. She maintained her ladylike composure, showing me a better example of how to enjoy my meal. She carefully dipped the spoon into her chili, pursed her lips to blow on each bite, and after eating it, dabbed her mouth with her napkin to make sure nothing was left behind. She sliced her cornbread with a knife and ate it in tiny bits. Everything about her was delicate and graceful.

After finishing my meal, she told me gently that I must wash my plate, spoon, fork, and cup, then put them away. I told her that Mama had taught me to do that before she'd died. Mother Lee was also impressed that I'd learned to cook by the age of five. While we talked, she pulled out a stepstool and helped me to not get dishwater on my clothing. While I was washing my dishes, Mother Lee stepped out to help another child. I waited for her as I finished drying my utensils and cup, so she could show me where everything went.

Rean came in and showed me where the bowl and spoon went, but the cups were high on a shelf. I asked Rean to help me put the cup away. She reached for my dishes to put them away for me, but Mother Lee interrupted us. "No, Rean, please show our Gail where to put her cup. She needs to learn to put away her own cup."

I did have to stand on a stool to put my cup away. That was the first night of many of putting away my own dishes and being guided in a loving way. Like with Mama and Daddy, I was sustained by a support system that was adequately teaching me to care for myself.

We had been at Childhaven only a few weeks when Daddy and Wayne came for a visit. I was more than excited to see them, but also confused. Had they come to take us somewhere else? I knew we couldn't stay with them. I didn't want to leave Childhaven.

He explained they had come because they were lonely for us, and he wanted to see where we would be living and how we were being taken care of. He was very pleased with all he saw and all he met.

I wondered why they couldn't stay. Daddy was relatively young and could work on the farm. All of us could take care of Wayne. But I didn't ask. It made me sad they had to leave.

Childhaven didn't accept children with discipline problems or disabilities. Later, I was told that they had explained all this to Daddy. At the time, I thought, *If they won't let Wayne into Childhaven, they might not let him into heaven either.*

Chapter 16

Home to Stay

"Home interprets heaven. Home is heaven for beginners."
—Charles Henry Parkhurst

The most remarkable thing about Childhaven in those early years was that it was usually full of music. We couldn't stop singing. No matter what room we were in, one of the children would start singing, then others would join in with perfect harmony.

"We're members of the Church of Christ," Mother Lee would say, "We've been harmonizing since before we could talk."

The Church of Christ never used instruments in its services, so we learned quickly how to join others in beautiful, melodious sound.

Most of the children who came were Southern, so, we'd sing traditional hymns that we had sung so often. Everyone seemed to know the words to the songs, and even if we didn't, most of them were repetitive, so we were able to catch on quickly.

Sometimes Daddy Brock would lead us in singing as we'd all sit on the porch together. Because the house was positioned on a hill, there was a glorious overlook of at least forty acres of grass, all farmland. There were 660 acres altogether.

To the side of the house was an old swimming pool that had been built in the 1800s. In the distance sat a large, gray rock barn and a tall grain silo. Because the yard was well kept, everything was fair game for exploration.

In the summers, the big children would help the little children catch lightning bugs in a jar for Mother Lee. She'd smile at her glowing lantern gift and place it on the porch for a while, before teaching us the value of setting the bugs free. We especially enjoyed it when she and Daddy Brock would play outside with us. They loved to do so—especially during winter.

Though Southern winters provided little in the way of snow, we celebrated a snowstorm during our eighth Christmas at Childhaven by building a snowman two stories high. The big boys got ladders. The adults helped us pack the snow tight for a sturdy head and body. We used a huge tablecloth to make the scarf. It is, to this day, the biggest thing I have ever seen made of snow. The townspeople of Cullman would drive by and step outside of their cars to watch us. They'd wave at us, and sometimes strike up a conversation.

The community of Cullman was very good to us. Because they loved decorating so much, they committed to a Christmas Parade of Homes each year that included Childhaven. The town donated all the garland, lights, and holiday knickknacks that were hung at our home. There was a five-piece electric candle set in every window.

The small reception room was decorated with a big tree. The older children, as time went on, got to go cut the tree and decorate it—a most exciting time.

On Christmas Eve, all the children would gather in that room to receive one gift. Later that night, I lay wide awake, in gratitude for the day. My mind drifted to Daddy. I wondered what he would say. Something inside me knew he would be happier than ever that we were happy. I whispered to the enchanted night: *Things are good here, Daddy. Merry Christmas.* Then I drifted off to sleep, confident that he had heard me.

The first Christmas, I thought that that was all there was to the holiday and was happy. But on Christmas morning, I awoke to a big box of wrapped presents. I ripped open my package with excitement.

Among the things I got was a doll. I had never really cared for dolls after I had left mine with Mama. I thought the doll's hair was too long, so I found some scissors and cut her hair badly, so it was very short. Mother Lee cried when she saw her. I never understood why, but I never cut a doll's hair again.

In the big box of presents were school clothes and jacks. I became very good at jacks. They were always more fun than dolls.

My first Christmas at Childhaven was the most jubilant experience I'd ever had. We were all grateful children who had been gifted a home for the holidays. *Santa* had come for each of us. He'd never visited my siblings and me but once. I wasn't sure what changed his mind, but I didn't care.

A Childhaven picture from about 1954 or 1955

At Childhaven, we were a unit bound by love and respect. We ate every meal together, and though we were separated by apartments, we almost always played together. But we didn't swim together. Boys swam with boys and girls swam with girls.

I was in second grade when I went to Childhaven. We had school friends who often visited after school. We all went to East Cullman Elementary, then with time and age—Cullman Middle School and High School when we got old enough.

Some of us babysat. Parents would bring their children to Childhaven. Sometimes we went to people's houses to take care of an older person or a sick child. If teenagers made their own money, they never had to contribute to household expenses. They got to keep it.

One thing Mother Lee and Daddy Brock took seriously was preparing us for further education. They wanted to see us do well for ourselves, so they were committed to ensuring we made good grades. They knew once we graduated from high school, we needed to either go to college (which most did) or get a job and be on our own as soon as possible. Some children went into the military.

When I arrived at Childhaven, I was grateful to be surrounded by family; the shared rooms made me feel less alone. But by the end of the year, there were so many children living at Childhaven that the oldest children were moved out of the nursery. I was moved into the apartment with the *big girls*. Because I was the oldest in the group, the young ones would paint my nails and roll my hair.

By the time I left Childhaven more than a decade later, there were children in every age bracket: elementary, middle, high school, and early college. The oldest child was twenty. The older children helped care for the younger ones.

A postcard from Childhaven

Chapter 17

A Child Left Behind

"Believe in yourself! Have faith in your abilities! Without a humble but reasonable confidence in your own powers you cannot be successful or happy."
—Norman Vincent Peale

I truly was *a child left behind* when it came to my schooling. In addition to growing up impoverished and transient, I had a difficult time keeping up with the other children in my class. It was the way of small, southern towns in the 1950s to join classes together depending on the size of each age group. My first school had two classrooms, a lunchroom, and two teachers. First through sixth grades were in one room and higher grades were in the other.

At Childhaven, we had everything from hopscotch to all kinds of made-up toys and games. We'd play on the swings, the slide, and the merry-go-round together. Sometimes, we'd play jump rope and sing songs—the way we did at home. One of my favorite times in elementary school was singing with Mr. Williamson and the glee club.

He asked me where I learned to sing. I told him Daddy loved singing songs. He used to take us in the car and play the radio for us. Then I told him about Childhaven and what Mother Lee had said, that members of the Church of Christ are born harmonizing. This made me wonder if Daddy's relationship with the church, although weak, might have been enough to influence his love of music.

Mr. Williamson told me to sing something familiar. I sang a hymn that the children all knew. He was so impressed that he had me perform by myself at a PTA meeting. This piqued my interest in the performance arts, so I began singing, acting, and trying out for the annual school plays.

I learned that while singing soprano came naturally to me—I was also gifted with the ability to sing alto. This made many of the other girls curious.

Several approached me, asking me if I could teach them to sing, but I wasn't yet fully aware of what I was doing.

It wasn't until Mr. Williamson broke down the process that I understood how neat it was that my voice had such versatility. I wondered if anyone else in our family had the same gift. In addition to vocal abilities, their talent for music seemed endless.

Daddy had a good voice and would harmonize with vocalists over the crackling radio. He also could carry a tune on the harmonica, which we children loved to listen to him play. You would have thought he was a celebrity in our household when he'd pull it out; he and Mama would sing familiar songs, and sometimes he'd just create a pleasant tune and we'd make up words all on our own.

Mama's daddy, Papaw, once made an instrument that impressed everyone in the family. He'd strung a dark green wooden box he'd painted that sounded just as good as a guitar. Though we rarely visited Mama's parents, on those rare family occasions all the male relatives would gather around him and sing along as he played. It'd always been the cheapest way to spend our time.

After Mr. Williamson mentioned my talents to Mother Lee and Daddy Brock, they decided to showcase the abilities of several of the other children. As a result, Childhaven hired a man to organize us into a chorus. A large group of us from Childhaven, about twenty children, were invited to sing at churches throughout Alabama. We'd get into our bus together and be shuttled out, usually right before a Southern picnic at a church building or nearby park.

Passersby would push their strollers up. Cars would stop. We'd get the attention of just about everybody—people were impressed by us. We were a diverse but polished-looking group who took pride in presenting ourselves as a family. When it was possible, Mother Lee and Daddy Brock would join us, gazing at us happily while we sang.

When I was an older teenager, we formed a Childhaven quartet, called the Havenetts. We went to Auburn University in Alabama for the 4-H competition. We went not just as Childhaven children, but as performers. On another occasion, we competed in a talent show when the fair came to town. The star was Brenda Lee. We won first place in both events.

Mother Lee had already bought us very cute outfits to wear because she was so confident we would win the seventy-five-dollar prize. She said, "When you win, we will pay for the dresses, and y'all can have what's left." We won the seventy-five dollars and had enough left for us to have a little spending money.

There was nothing that made me feel closer to Mama and Daddy than singing. Even if they weren't physically present with us, it was as if I could feel them there, celebrating that we were in a season of happiness—*finally*.

By third grade, I'd fallen even more in love with Childhaven. I was enjoying our bedroom with other girls and was thrilled to have so many children around. That was, until one of us got sick. It never mattered that we were quarantined off to some degree. If one of us fell ill, especially the younger ones, it was almost guaranteed that the rest of the house would catch it. In the cold months, we'd carry in the flu, and it'd circulate through the nursery like a plague before we'd even realized we'd let it in.

Don was in the third grade when he got the measles, and they just wouldn't go away. He would get over them and then have them again. Everybody was getting measles back then since they didn't have shots. They finally determined that he wasn't *getting* measles, he was getting an *allergic reaction to measles*. He would get around another child that had measles and he would break out. Because he was sick so much that year, he had to repeat the third grade, making him and Brenda in the same grade for the rest of school.

Daddy and I were stunned when, at age eight, Don's eyes went from cornflower blue to chocolate brown, possibly as a reaction to his illness. He was an entirely new version of himself, and it took some adjusting to. But it wasn't long before he was confident with his new look.

When I became sick with no sign of sickness spreading throughout the rest of Childhaven, I was surprised. It began with a raw throat that led to significant sinus drainage, especially at night. I was so miserable I'd try to occupy myself with anything, but nothing could keep my mind off the pain that kept me from sleeping. Soon, I developed blisters all over my lips, face, and neck. It hurt to breathe, to swallow, to move. I started losing weight quickly due to never being hungry; the pain of eating wasn't worth suffering through a spoonful of hot soup or parting my lips to chew.

Mother Lee exhausted herself taking me to doctors, but none could determine what was wrong with me. Because none of the other children were falling ill, they assumed it wasn't highly contagious, which led them to believe it had more to do with a weakened immune system.

Though it was obvious to the doctors my illness was mouth-related, they didn't realize how bad things had gotten in my lungs. Dr. Barrett, who was a member of the Childhaven Board of Trustees, became determined to figure out what was wrong with me.

We drove forty miles to his private hospital in Decatur, Alabama, a facility that had just a few beds. He examined me and diagnosed what no doctor had discovered up to that point: I had a severe case of strep throat which had progressed to strep lung because it hadn't been treated. He treated me with antibiotics, not realizing we were only at the beginning of my troubles.

A local physician, Dr. Clemons, insisted I needed my tonsils out as the strep had infected them, and was infecting my entire body. After they were removed, I ran a high fever and had to stay in the hospital for ten more days to ensure I was all right. It was such an ordeal that by the time I was better, I was ready to be home at Childhaven, even if I was secluded in a little room in the nursery for a short period of time.

I was lavished with many nice gifts from Daddy Brock and Mother Lee upon my return.

And even throughout my stay at the hospitals they'd roam the halls, worried sick, even though they were never allowed to come in to see me. When the nurses would open the door to usher in food trays, I'd sometimes get a glimpse of one of them outside and feel flooded with warmth. They helped me get around *the rules* when it came to eating while recovering. Knowing I absolutely hated milk, Mother Lee insisted I not have any. I'd never been a huge fan of dairy, (except for ice cream, and I was picky about that).

They spoiled me as best they could while I was bedridden. I always felt it, even if they couldn't be in the same room with me. They provided one of my greatest sources of entertainment: a booklet with embossed pictures. If I ran a flattened pencil over the pages, things appeared, like faces, animals, and landscape scenes. I was also given Dot to Dots, crossword puzzles, and coloring books.

Though I'd been away from Don and Brenda many times, I hadn't expected them to grow so tall while I was away. They wrapped me up with hugs for the longest time, and told me they'd missed me, having hung onto every word of Daddy Brock's updates about my health.

When I finally returned to school after my sickness, it felt strange to be around the other children. By that time, third grade had started. My teacher's name was Mrs. McFearson. With the knowledge that I was still recovering, she was patient with me in every area but one: drinking milk. I still refused to drink it. Absolutely refused. I hated the taste of it, I could hardly swallow it, and I outsmarted her attempts to get me to drink it. Nothing worked and nothing ever would.

Finally, despite the school's fears that I would lose the nourishment I needed to continue healing, they decided to order me orange juice from the milkman. Every day after that, when everyone else would get their tiny carton of milk, I would receive orange juice. It was the most delicious treat in the world except Nehi grape. It also made me feel special for the first time in my school years, because I was the only one who had it. To everyone's delight, it nourished my body just enough to get me back outside playing as hard as I could. I was so excited to be back on the playground and I got comfortable around all the children rather quickly.

Through our wily adventures, the children of Childhaven and I built outstanding memories together, some of which were more hysterical than others.

As I got older, I got closer to some of the more *mischievous* children. *Mischief*, in our home, was always safe and all in good fun. We'd poke lighthearted jokes at each other, and never thought up anything too bad, except for one time.

We'd about had our fill of sissy Viola. To be fair, we'd all seen our parents either do bad things or suffer from unfortunate circumstances. Viola had seen her daddy cut her mother's throat—something no child should ever have to witness. But she'd always used her past as a way of getting out of *helping* around the house—and especially with the chickens—because she was *terrified of blood*. We'd all seen blood, so we just rolled our eyes at her.

In retrospect, it's fair to assume Viola might have had a true phobia. In the 1950s, that wasn't even a concept. She was incredibly afraid of *a lot* of things. At night, she'd compulsively look under the bed for the bogeyman and search the closet for monsters. The rest of us had overcome awful things too. Some children had lost both parents. Some had been sold for sex. Some had been outright abandoned. But we all had adjusted well. Quite frankly, we were sick of it. Because instead of doing chores, she got to sit and watch television.

If Viola was looking for the bogeyman, we were going to make sure she found him. So, one day, a group of us got some old boy's clothes: overalls, a long-sleeve shirt, and a hat. We used an old stuffed stocking for the head, and I painted a face on it. We were pleased with our work. It looked pretty good.

We opened her closet curtain, pushed her clothes to one side, propped up the dummy, then waited for her to find it. When we finally heard the loudest screams imaginable, we began laughing so hard that our sides hurt. Our housemother came running in to comfort Viola. To this day, I believe she was holding back a smile as she told us we were in *big trouble*.

The next day, Daddy Brock called us out on the big front porch. There we were met by a burly policeman. First, we were shamed for what we had done, but were then given a chance to speak. Instead of taking responsibility, we decided to keep a united front, and we blamed Viola herself for being such a scaredy-cat. Then the policeman spoke to our point, "You know that if Viola had been *scared to death,* you'd all go to prison for the rest of your lives, right?"

We snickered until his voice got firmer.

"Yes sir," one of the older girls finally said.

"That's what I like to hear," the police officer continued. "Act like you belong to somebody," he said. "It's time to grow up!"

I smiled to myself knowing it was *because* I belonged to someone that the opposite was true. I was in no way ready to grow up. I was going to relish my years at Childhaven for as long as possible.

Because I loved playing ball with the boys at Childhaven, I'd developed a love for competitive sports. If there was a sport, I played it. While the other girls would sit, playing with dolls, I wanted to rough up my knees, run through the wild air, and *win*. I loved to win.

This experience made me especially good at games with hand-eye coordination; it even made me better at jacks, which I enjoyed playing all by myself. I was also very good at kickball. I loved the way the big rubber ball would hit the tip of my toe and bounce high up in the air. I had become tall for my age and I could send it soaring across the playground over everyone's heads.

Thinking the rules would be similar to softball, I gave all kinds of ball a try. Though I wasn't as strong as the boys, I could swing really high on the swing set, which made the boys think I was good at it. They were hesitant to let me join in their fun, but two boys from the home finally invited me to play with them.

Van and Raymond were talented little leaguers who were always competing with each other. Their favorite thing was to stand on the wooden planks and pump their feet hard on the swing set, trying to make it go all the way around. They were courageous and physically capable, but I never once thought they were better than me at anything they did. I'd watch their efforts to get as high as they could and think, *I bet I can swing higher than that.* I'd practice on my own a lot, even while wearing a dress. But I was so light my feet would leave the swing in midair and I'd panic. I could never fully commit to going higher than that. The falling sensation always became too overwhelming.

Still, I loved swinging, and I could spend hours in the sun, letting my body be enveloped by the bright, blue sky. I especially loved the months of September and October when the varying hues of green would transition into brilliant oranges, reds, and yellows. To me, the world looked like a paint palette, especially after seeing only the bland inside of a hospital room for several weeks.

On one occasion, we were having a classroom discussion on colors. Soon, we stumbled onto the *rules* about colors in fashion. Mrs. Chapman, my second-grade teacher, went on about how it would never be proper to wear navy and black together, or black and brown. She asked the class what combinations they thought looked best when worn together. I peered out across the schoolyard, watching the sun melt down on the soft earth and front flowerbed. It was so beautiful I wanted to wrap the day around me like a fabulous cape. The outside sky was blue, the grass a bright green.

I raised my hand to answer her question and enthusiastically said, “Blue and green!”

To my surprise, she responded, “No, Gail, absolutely not. Those colors should never be worn together.”

I was confused and angry. I felt she was criticizing God for putting the colors together. *Wasn’t Mrs. Chapman supposed to be the creative one?* She’d always inspired us to think for ourselves and made sure that we felt supported and confident in presenting our opinions. To experience her objection to something I felt so strongly about meant one thing: I had to prove her wrong.

Later that day, we were to take out our crayons and draw a scene of our own choosing. I had three things working in my favor: my knack for the arts, my own stubbornness, and the fact that I was determined to prove a point. So, I thought of the most beautiful scene I could think of. I closed my eyes and remembered myself standing in front of my bedroom window at the lake house. I pictured twilight, and how it felt to look out over the waters, when even the air in front of me was blue, and it made the blades of grass near the lake an even richer green.

I put my crayon to the paper and drew what I saw. Careful with the details, I poured my heart into it. As minutes ticked on, I lost myself in a memory. I imagined Mama standing out by the lake the first time she saw me swimming. I saw Wayne's wheelchair near the bank, while Daddy carried his body out to enjoy the water. I remembered the ripples on the lake when Daddy and I skipped smooth stones across it—and I felt all of them.

I drew tall mountains in the distance, complete with the silhouettes of trees. Every inch of paper that wasn't water and sky, I colored green. Every inch of paper that wasn't grass or foliage, I colored blue.

Right before the sound of the bell, Mrs. Chapman collected my paper. Impressed, she looked at me with kind, remorseful eyes and held my drawing up for the class.

"I was wrong," she said, "Gail knew better than me. Blue and green go together perfectly," she said with the slightest smile.

"Yes, they do," I agreed, feeling confident and smart.

Perfectly.

Gail in seventh grade

Chapter 18

The Memories of Childhaven, a Home for Fortunate Children

"The steadfast love of the LORD never ceases; his mercies never come to an end;
they are new every morning; great is your faithfulness."
—Lamentations 3:22-23

Because of my unfortunate delays in being properly educated, my teachers thought it would be best if I repeated second grade. At nine years old, I was put in a mixed class of second and third graders so I could also start doing third-grade work.

I was sad at first, afraid it *meant* something about my intelligence. But Mother Lee and Daddy Brock insisted it had nothing to do with me. They both comforted me, and affirmed that I was smart, even though learning to read was a struggle for me. I felt left out because I loved stories, but they seemed out of reach to me. I kept thinking that reading would come more easily to me at some point, not knowing at the time, I was struggling with dyslexia.

Every day, Mrs. Chapman read to us. Our first book was *Charlotte's Web,* our second was *Little Britches*. I had never been read to before but hearing the stories allowed me to imagine everything with clarity and excitement. I liked it, and I wanted to stay in those moments forever.

By the time I reached third grade, the coursework was easier. Mrs. McFearson noticed my improvement and told Mrs. Chapman, who stopped me in the hall and told me she was proud of me. It was difficult to part from Mrs. McFearson because we'd established trust and a routine. But by our final months together, I was ready to move on to fourth grade with a new classroom, new coursework, and new teacher, Mrs. Thompson.

I knew a little about Mrs. Thompson. She went to church with me. She was a decent teacher, and I liked her most of the time. But there were other times when she put me on the spot or said hurtful things, taking the liberty of speaking her mind, because she knew me outside of school. On one occasion, she asked what the abbreviation "St." stood for. One student said, "street." I said, "saint," having heard the disciples referred to as *saints*: Saint Peter, Saint John, Saint Matthew.

Mrs. Thompson snapped at me, "Absolutely not—you should know better than that." I didn't understand at the time what she was referring to—that no person should be called a saint (but she was wrong). These are formalities I didn't understand because I hadn't grown up in the church. To my dismay, it wasn't the first or the last time I would be embarrassed by her.

For reasons I could never explain, I frequently had headaches. I'd become moody, lethargic, and nauseous. When Mrs. Thompson would ask me what was wrong, I would tell her, “I think I need to go to the office. I have a headache.”

She’d shush me, telling me *children were too young to have headaches,* as if I didn’t know what I was talking about.

I’d stubbornly respond, “It sure feels like a headache to me. I think it’s going to rain in a little while. When it does rain, my head will stop hurting.”

“It doesn’t even look like rain outside,” she’d respond, then go about her teaching as my temples throbbed worse and worse. Finally, the sky would open up into a downpour. And when it did, the tension in my head, jaw, and neck would release. Mrs. Thompson would always be shocked by my prediction. After it happened several times, she stopped doubting me. Decades later, doctors would discover the symptoms of children who suffer from barometric pressure headaches. I was one of them. It was fitting because I was sensitive to everything, highly empathic, attuned, and creative.

Because I was artistic and became bored with Mrs. Thompson’s droning, I did a lot of drawing in her class on anything I could find: desks, homework pages, my books, and unlined three-by-five cards.

It was around this time that I began writing poetry. Completely unprompted stanzas just started pouring out of me. Some rhymed, but the more liberating ones didn't. Through writing, I began processing all kinds of things: cheerful things, like Childhaven, and not-so-cheerful things, like missing Mama and Daddy and Wayne. I never showed these poems to anyone. But I did like the way they sounded when I read them to myself.

Soon, I'd receive a life-changing gift, especially for a young girl.

I had strong teeth, but they protruded. So, when I was thirteen years old, I became the first child in town to wear braces.

There were two or three dentists in town who worked on all the children. I was my orthodontist's very first patient. He had been a regular dentist, but when he was an older man, he'd gone back to school to learn orthodontics. I wore braces for six years. I got them removed when I was a senior in high school. By then, it became a popular thing to do for children who had crooked teeth. I was very pleased with the results.

Ronnie, my good friend from Childhaven, was the second child to have braces.

By the time I was fifteen, I'd bonded with the older girls at Childhaven. I had *sisters*—sisters who took up for me in school, taught me how to style my hair just right, told me secrets about *boys*, and helped me with my English homework.

By seventh grade, I was prepared to make the dreaded adjustment of going to different classrooms with a different set of teachers. Childhaven had prepared me for *all kinds* of situations. This empowered me to do things I loved and to embrace variety. Because singing was still important to me, I tried out for the school chorus and was accepted. I'd been in glee club in elementary school from grades two to six. I also started going to 4-H club, in part to get out of class, but also because I was genuinely enjoying learning about agriculture.

Meanwhile, Childhaven was growing rapidly. Soon, ten more families had joined the household, an addition of at least forty children. The nursery remained a haven for the very young. Mother Lee and Daddy Brock added two more apartments to the second story and moved out of their apartment to a new house built for them across the road. Their old living quarters were given to the middle school girls so they would have more space to get ready with more privacy. A separate upstairs apartment was restored for the older children. That is where I found myself learning from all the other girls, and my beloved housemother. My favorite was Aunt Anna.

We girls naturally bonded with each other. All children and adults ate meals at the same time in the dining room. We'd alternate roles: some girls would help prepare food, and some would help clean up after. We would do dishes, clear the tables, and put away the leftovers. We were also taught to do household chores: keeping our clothes laundered, folded, and put away; making sure our beds were made each morning; and ensuring all our belongings stayed tidy.

Each person's room had three to four other children in it. Because we genuinely enjoyed each other's company, we got along well. We didn't argue. We shared. We spent quality time together. And we tried to help each other the best we could.

While it was rare, every once in a while, a child at Childhaven would go back home to their families.

We had brothers who were teenagers. Their family wanted them back. Although the boys could have lived at Childhaven for the rest of their lives, the family had a court order to regain custody of them. Mother Lee said that the family wanted them back because they were old enough to go to work. They ran away so their family couldn't get them.

The younger brother was rounded up somehow. A police officer put him in the backseat of his car. He slid across, opened the other door, and ran away again. He just did not want to go. Finally, the younger of the two was returned home to his family, crying as he left. But the older brother was still unaccounted for.

At Childhaven, we had a piano that was catty-cornered in the dining room. We hid that other boy behind that piano. We got him some pillows and things to make him more comfortable. Some of the boys were bringing clothes for him to change into. When nobody was around, he would sneak out and go to the bathroom that was normally reserved for guests and clean up and put on clean clothes. Nobody wanted to see him go. For days and days, we made sure he was fed. We would come play the piano and visit with him.

Mother Lee figured it out. She said, "You girls just don't play the piano that much." He had to go. It was a very sad day for a lot of us because we liked the brothers a lot. They loved being at Childhaven.

Though most of the children at Childhaven never got visits from family, Daddy would come to see Don, Brenda, and me, always bringing Wayne with him. Once my Aunt Dollie and one of Daddy's relatives came to Childhaven to visit us at the same time. We got more visits from family than most of the children at Childhaven.

When Daddy visited, we'd savor everything about him. We'd eat lunch with him, tell him about school, and catch up with our big brother. Every time

Daddy saw us, he'd be amazed at how old we'd gotten, and we'd be sad that his face had more lines than before. He was looking older too.

He was also settling in with Frances, his second wife. She'd been a longtime family friend and neighbor who had gotten close to Daddy after her husband had been tragically killed. I was sixteen when they married. After they married, he began raising her four children with her in a three-bedroom house. We would visit Daddy and Wayne for several weeks in the summer, particularly as we got older. Frances's oldest daughter, who was my age, was fickle and competitive. When we'd attempt to get along through a simple tabletop game or through playing Old Maid, we'd just get in spats.

At one point, there was a conversation on whether Don, Brenda, and I should be returned to Daddy. He had gone to a judge to get permission. A man from the Welfare Department came to me and said, "Your daddy would like you all to come back home to live with him. He's got a job, a house, a wife, and he's got enough money. He can take care of you."

At sixteen, I was nearly grown, and Brenda and Don weren't far behind. I thought about the poverty in my past with four children living in the same house, and compared it to what I already had, and what I knew was in the future with eight children in one house. No one involved could see the ten of us living comfortably in such close quarters and having enough food and clothing to be satisfied.

I knew that Don, Brenda, and I wouldn't be able to pursue our college education if we moved back in with Daddy. We'd have to get jobs instead to help pay for household expenses and then save up to get a place to live. But we already had all of that where we were. Plus, Don, Brenda, and I were truly happy.

So, I told the man that I didn't want us to do that. Then I wrote Daddy a really long letter and explained my thinking. I never mentioned it to Don and Brenda because I felt, as the oldest, I was able to speak for all our best interests.

Frances told me later that when Daddy read the letter, he cried a little bit. But then he said, "Somebody has done a good job raising this girl."

Daddy saw that we had everything we needed except for him: a loving home, fantastic friends, and the chance to get a great education. He loved us enough to let us go live happy lives. Though it was sad, we children stayed.

It was probably twenty years later that I told Brenda and Don the whole story. They were very mad at me—for about ten minutes. They thought that they should have been in on the decision, but then they both said, "We would have said the same thing."

One of the best treats the people of Cullman gave to Childhaven was free admission to the local movie theater for all the children. We'd tag along with the houseparents or older children, and if we had our own money, we could buy Cokes, popcorn, or candy. After sharing our snacks with our own sisters and brothers, it always felt like the biggest treat—to recline in dark, cushioned seats on Friday night, the paths illuminated by running neon lights leading up to the tiny projection booth in the back.

Mother Lee and Daddy Brock loved that our community took such good care of us. But they wanted to go above and beyond to empower us with the life skills we would need to thrive in the world.

Some of those were refined through education, some through chores, and others through agriculture and food preparation skills. Daddy Brock taught us about going back to the earth to raise our food, through working with crops, dairy, and maintaining a garden.

As children, we were taught how to grow our own food. We took great delight in planting seeds, watching them sprout, then cutting them for meals. It taught us the value of hard work, and how to nourish our bodies from something we'd sown with our hands.

The gardens at Childhaven were huge. The boys mostly planted and took care of the crops while the girls worked inside slicing, storing, and freezing. Nearby landowners loved hosting us. They'd invite us to come and pick fruit, which was always a delight for us. It always felt like an exploration, never work to me.

We had more dairy cows than we could even keep track of. The boys were taught to milk cows. They teased us girls when we couldn't. (Looking back, I think they were giving us cows that had already been milked.) We never had to buy milk or beef. Later, we had automatic milkers and a pasteurizing plant. We also used some of the cows for meat. Cows were carried to the butchers. We grew all our own hay, bailed it, and stored it in a stone barn on the property that was well over one hundred years old. We also sold our own leftover milk to Sealtest Dairy.

Today, the government has made the sweeter parts of Childhaven *illegal*. We called it *farming,* they call it *child labor*.

We were taught to care for the animals, and this included the horses that people of Cullman boarded at Childhaven. We were allowed to ride them if we wanted to. We also had our own horse named Charlie Boy. Because it was good for them to be ridden, we were taught proper horse care and riding technique.

At one time, we had our own little zoo. It was in the outdoor kitchen that was used for cooking when it was the Odd Fellows home. Food was brought in from there to the main building.

We had one squirrel that was kept in a large cage. I always thought it needed to be outdoors. We had parakeets, and some snakes, and rabbits, animals we found nearby. Two boys, Van and Raymond, even had a worm bed and people would come and buy worms from them. A flying squirrel that belonged to Daddy Brock was my favorite.

At one point a bull named "16 Tons" lived at Childhaven. He was gentle and big. A doctor in Birmingham and the University of Auburn had pooled $16,000 to purchase him. He lived part time at Childhaven and part time at University of Auburn. Auburn used the bull for artificial insemination research. It was a fairly new process, and they had no idea what it would yield.

Not long after that we had one red bull with a bad temperament that posed a threat to every animal on the property. After it attacked one of the horses and charged at some of the children, they had to put it down.

The children were relieved to see the demise of the bull. We were very protective of our animals. Most of us had never had pets before. We loved them with a gratitude that was so deep. We took great pride in anything we were given. This applied to our personal belongings as well.

Soon, my friend Pat and I came up with an idea to prove we were as good as the boys when it came to farm work.

Pat and I were physically the exact opposite: she was the shortest girl, and I was the tallest. Sometimes we would go and help the boys throw the square bales of hay up into the truck bed. It probably wasn't the best thing to have lifted that much. We didn't do it every day, but we did it enough to earn their respect and to get a good workout. Now I know what it's like to pitch hay, and I never want to do it again.

We also housed 100,000 chickens in five separate brooder houses. Not only did we save money by raising our own chickens to eat, but we also made money by selling the rest. At one point, Pat and I asked to help tend to a house that had 20,000 baby chicks in it. Because those tasks were usually given to the boys, again, we wanted to prove we could do an even better job. In retrospect, I can't say why we were so eager, since it meant we had to be up at dawn on school days.

The tending itself was very easy. We poured large bags of feed into a big bin, then turned on a switch. A chain sifted through the food bin, then carried feed around the building to all the feeding troughs. Watering the chicks was just as simple.

Just like people, some chickens were naturally wild, and they would pick at other chickens. When we spotted one like that, we had to put *glasses* on them. We called them glasses, but they were more like blinders that went over their eyes, secured by a little pin through their beak. With blinders on, they can see food underneath, but can't see another chicken to pick at it.

We also had to *stir* the chickens twice per day in addition to feeding them twice per day. Stirring them consisted of walking through the chicken house to make sure there was not a cluster of birds in a corner that could potentially cause one of them to get smothered.

Pat and I were proud of the work we'd done, and when they finally sold that house full of chickens, our chickens weighed more than any Childhaven had ever sold. Of course, after doing such a good job on our first round of tending to the chickens, we were asked to do it again. We said *no thank you,* as we'd just been out to prove a point. Namely to ourselves.

Catching chickens for sale was an adventure in and of itself.

I actually looked forward to it. It had to be done on a Friday night because chickens can only be easily caught at night, as they can't see in the dark. The older boys and girls in high school would put on old clothes, then meet at the chicken house to go work. When we got there, a large truck full of crates would be waiting. They'd pull the crates off the truck, then we'd go into the pitch-black chicken house to *feel* for the chicken's legs. Once our hands grazed a leg, we'd pick it up. They'd squawk and flap like crazy, which was always a little scary at first, but became funnier and easier to manage as we went. We'd grab a bundle, then carry them upside down over to older boys who would crate sixteen chickens at once.

Each chicken weighed around three to five pounds, so most of us could catch eight at a time. Some girls would pair up and catch four each. It was a huge endeavor that took us until the wee hours of the morning.

When our task was over, we would go to a restaurant that would stay open for us. It was a huge treat. We could order anything we wanted. Then we would go home, bathe, and go to bed. We could sleep as late as we wanted. It was one of the most sacred bonding experiences of our childhood, something I miss even to this day when I see a chicken house.

We also caught and killed chickens that were kept for us. The boys would catch the chickens and place them in a large crate with a door on top to secure them, while the girls would prepare a gigantic cast iron pot filled with water that sat on a rack. Beneath the pot was a stack of firewood for boiling the water. Before the chickens were killed, the water had to be scalding hot, and its temperature needed to be maintained through the process.

Both the boys and girls helped with the killing. There were two ways to do this: one was to chop its head off, and the other was to hold the chicken by the head, then sling the chicken ‘round and ‘round, until its neck was *wrung* and severed from its body.

Most of us chose the first option. Out back, we had a large stump for chopping. In the stump were two large nails that were about an inch apart—just enough space to brace the chicken's neck.

One child would hold the chicken by both feet and slam it onto the stump, aiming to place its neck between the two nails. If they missed the first time, they'd just place the head in the appropriate position. One child would hold the feet to stretch the neck. Then with a hatchet, we would chop off the chicken's head and throw it to the ground. I'd never understood the phrase, "running around like a chicken with your head cut off" until I saw it for myself.

Often there would be a dozen or more chickens running around headless. When one would finally fall dead, it was picked up and dipped into the hot water for a couple of minutes. The scalding water made the feathers come out easily. Everyone not killing had to pluck feathers. Every so often, someone would come and get the plucked chickens and take them to the kitchen, where some adults would gut and cut up the chicken, wrap it in freezer paper, and put it in the great freezer.

And that was a typical Friday night and Saturday in my childhood home—the pinnacle of adventure. The hallmark of Childhaven, where the motto was **"A Home for Fortunate Children."** I felt incredibly fortunate.

Mother Lee was intentional about teaching us proper autonomy *and* about sharing. She acknowledged that most of us would struggle with matters of ownership, as we'd come from impoverished homes. Abusive, neglectful circumstances. We'd never had our own toys before. But the message of the home was that it was healthy and joyful to give freely; it did not mean we would go *without*. So, we shared for the right reasons, and were respectful of each other's belongings.

Unfortunately, we were about to learn that one of the board members hadn't learned this lesson and had been extremely disrespectful to several children.

One very wealthy unmarried man was on our board of trustees. Every once in a while, he would bring many gallons of ice cream to Childhaven and we would have a big ice cream party. Everybody looked forward to his coming because we got ice cream. After the party, he would take two or three little boys home with him on Friday for the weekend, bringing them back on Sunday. I was too young to even think that way, but the adults should have known better.

One time he took my friend Paul home with him. Paul and I were in the same grade at school in elementary. We had become good friends, maybe even best friends.

When the man started to molest him, Paul got away from him somehow. Paul went to the room that the man had given him, climbed out the window, and ran away. When he hit a nearby road, he started walking in the direction of what he thought was Childhaven.

Paul had escaped on Friday afternoon, but the man did not report him missing until Sunday morning. Finally, a bulletin came across the radio: "Missing boy from Childhaven," with Paul's description.

A woman who happened to be a member of the Church of Christ heard the radio report. She pulled off the side of the road and prayed that someone would find him. Then she started her car again and headed to church. When she went around the curve, there was

Paul. She pulled over and asked, "Are you Paul from Childhaven?"

And he said, "Yes."

"I'll take you home," she offered. She brought him back home to Childhaven.

Paul told Daddy Brock what happened. He immediately called a meeting of the board of directors. When all were there but this man, there was a huge scene on our big front porch. We all had our windows up but all we could hear was loud noises and yelling. It scared us children. The tension and stress of knowing what had happened to Paul—perpetrated by a Christian board member—caused Daddy Brock to have a heart attack and he almost died.

Because of that meeting and the interrogations of children that followed, it was soon discovered that the man was also on the board at two other orphan homes. He was doing the same thing to the children at those two places. When some of the other boys were questioned, they told what had happened, too young to know it was wrong.

People weren't punished back then about things like they are now (even now sometimes people aren't punished the way they should be), but I can't take care of the whole world. I don't know if the man had to go to jail, but at least he was removed from the boards.

After we were in high school, Paul and I would sometimes walk home instead of riding our bus. We were something like kindred spirits. I felt safe with Paul if someone unwelcome should approach us. We would take our time and venture off the road to see what we might find. Sometimes he would come to my room. We would climb out the window and sit on the roof to a porch on the lower floor. (It was against the rules, but we never got in trouble for it.)

Off and on after we were both married with families, he would call, and we'd talk for an hour or more.

One Sunday, Jerrie was preaching at the church where Paul attended. I didn't know Paul was a member there. As ladies do, I was standing in a long line waiting for my turn in the restroom, when I heard a commotion. I heard a male voice call out, "Gail. Gail!" It was Paul looking for me.

As I'm writing this, Paul is very sick with COVID-19. We're praying for a complete recovery.

Charles Albert Tindley wrote the lyrics to "Stand by Me" in 1905. I first heard it sung by Elvis when I was still in high school. It starts, "When the storms of life are raging, stand by me." I liked the song, but I thought it would be better if it said, "When the storms of life were raging, you stood by me," referring to how God was always with us. So, I rewrote the whole song in past tense. I guess when He was standing by me, I didn't know it. I still like my version better, but it would be harder to set to music. I still hear people or groups singing it, and I wish they understood He already had.

Aunt Winnie Smith, one of the houseparents, was a special lady to us all. She was old and wise. I'm not sure if she was taking care of us or if we were taking care of her. Her job was as a substitute. When some other adult needed a day off or wasn't feeling well, she would do their job.

In the spirit of good music, Aunt Winnie Smith wrote lyrics about Childhaven to the tune of "When It's Springtime in the Rockies." They went:

> When it's springtime at Childhaven
> The whole world is bright and gay
> And we are all so happy as we sing and work and play.
> We all love Daddy Brock and Mother Lee as well
> And all of our dear house parents for they are really swell.

While springtime in Alabama was beautiful, the summers could be brutally hot. The summer I was sixteen years old, there was a drought in Alabama. I guess we didn't know how badly it had affected us all, until the day it poured rain. It was the girls' time to swim. We were on our way from the big house when it started.

We threw off our robes (which was against the rules) and began yelling and prancing around like thirsty animals running to a watering hole. It was hot! And the rain felt wonderful. There was no lightning, so we went on into the pool. When we finally came in from the pool, Aunt Winnie Smith said, "If I had known how wonderful the rain would feel, I would have prayed for it earlier." She did take credit for it happening.

The old swimming pool at Childhaven, previously the Odd Fellows Home

The swimming pool now

I never wanted to displease my caretakers or dishonor myself. But I did once.

When I was 16, some of us Childhaven children had run into some school friends in town, probably 10 of us altogether. Someone suggested we all steal something. I was horrified at the suggestion and said, "No thanks."

They began to take things like gum and candy bars from store to store. Everyone had something but me. "I'm not going to," I said.

They called me "Goody Two Shoes," and "chicken," making clucking sounds. I still resisted. They still made fun.

Finally, I decided that *if I'm going to do this, I'm going to do it right.* Just then, we walked past a jewelry store. It felt like someone else was in my body. I opened the door and picked up the closest thing at hand, an expensive bracelet.

I was suddenly the hero, being slapped on the back and praised. I immediately wanted to turn back. I thought I could put it back as easily as I took it. But we walked on.

I was so angry and disappointed in myself, so I told my roommates. They couldn't believe I had done such a thing. I tried to sleep but couldn't. So, I got up and wrote Daddy Brock a letter telling him what I had done, asking him to take me back to the store to return the bracelet. I knew he would be disappointed. I also knew he would take me. I put the letter in his mailbox.

That morning he called me to his office. We talked and he was kind. I got dressed and we went to the store, bracelet in hand. He had already called the owner to let him know we were coming.

The owner received us into his office. I was crying. I hated looking the man in the eye, but I did. He was also very kind. He wished more people would return what they had taken.

I couldn't look at Daddy Brock, as I thought he was crying. The bracelet was expensive. The shop owner wanted me to keep it to remind me to never do anything like this again. I didn't need the bracelet to do that, but he insisted I keep it.

As we left, the store owner hugged me. Daddy Brock hugged me, too, and he told me he was proud of me. He *had* been crying.

I took the bracelet and threw it as far back in my closet as I could. I never wore it and finally gave it to Goodwill.

The bracelet was never mentioned again.

Chapter 19

Baby Jan

Too often we underestimate the power of a touch, a smile, a kind word, a listening ear, an honest compliment, or the smallest act of caring, all of which have the potential to turn a life around."
—Leo Buscaglia (Dr. Love, motivational speaker)

While all of us older children were dedicated to Childhaven, I had a vested interest in *giving back,* as our home had given so much to me. This meant I went above and beyond to nurture the younger children who came to live with us. After all, I'd helped Don and Brenda adapt, and by my high school years, I'd seen children in various stages of pain and grief. I'd taken on the philosophy of Mother Lee and Daddy Brock, that all children were worthy of love, and worthy of learning how to take care of themselves.

I took chores seriously. It was joyous for me to help take care of young children. I was absorbing as much of Childhaven as I possibly could. While my grades were fair, I enjoyed sports, singing, and theater. I knew it would be only four short years before I would go off into the world, and I wanted to savor every second.

In my high school years, Mother Lee and Daddy Brock put me to work in the office at Childhaven. Every Sunday, we had visitors—people from the community, friends, and church members, curious about where their money was going.

When we were little, adults took care of greeting visitors. As we grew and got more responsible, we older girls would have this duty, a couple each Sunday. The ones on duty would go quickly after church and eat dinner before the others to be ready. We called it, "showing people around." We all looked forward to it being our turn because people often gave us a dollar or more. We never asked for money, because we would have been in big trouble.

This particular Sunday, my friend Pat and I were ready for visitors. I had just gotten to the lobby to take my place when a young couple with a baby came in. The doors were never locked in those days, so people came and went as they pleased. The couple had blank looks on their faces as if they were very lost. The baby's head was on the lady's shoulders, but when she turned and saw me, she literally leaped from her arms to mine. She took me by such surprise that I barely caught her. She clung to me as if I were someone she knew. Immediately, I smelled a horrible odor coming from her.

Pat tried to take her, but she clung to me tighter and screamed an almost deafening scream. Mother Lee, noticing something strange happening, came to investigate.

The story was that the young couple had married the previous Sunday. This Sunday, when they came home from church, they found this baby in a box on their porch. A note said, "Please take care of me. My name is Jan." It was about the saddest story I had ever heard.

The man said, "We just can't take care of her and thought it best to bring her here." Mother Lee and

Daddy Brock told them we could take her. They would call the Child Welfare Department tomorrow. They left relieved, knowing her needs would be taken care of.

Before she left, the lady said, "I think she might be hurt."

We had some bathrooms that had bathtubs built on blocks so adults could stand to bathe the little ones. Mother Lee told me to give Jan a much-needed bath, since I was the only one she would allow to touch her.

She had a little dress on and very soiled diaper. The couple had stopped and bought her a pink coat. It was winter. Mother Lee thought she knew where some diapers were. There were no children young enough for them. The dress was stuck to Jan's flesh, so I ran a few inches of warm water in the tub.

Dinner was over. The other girls had circled around us out of curiosity. I started taking off her diaper—gently, fearing poop would go everywhere. It was very full and very smelly. There was so much in her diaper I couldn't see her skin. I tried wiping some before I put her in the water. Some was so old it was crusty and stuck to her skin.

She had stopped screaming and seemed curious about what was happening to her. I laid her in the warm water with her dress still on so the water would release her dress from her skin. I was trying to wash the feces off her and soon realized part of it was scabs. Once I got her bottom clean, I saw that everywhere the diaper touched was a solid sore. Her privates were swollen and scabby. After soaking in water, her dress had loosened from her flesh. When I pulled it off, I could see why it had been stuck. There were four deep cuts or scratches across her chest. The scratches were scabbed over with some infection on the edges, and very swollen and red all around.

One of the other girls brought me a cup to help me wash her. I poured the water over her chest carefully, then gently massaged her head and rinsed her hair. She seemed to like the water, so I tended to her longer.

I bathed her for at least thirty minutes, hoping I could wash away the terrible things that had happened to her. I also figured it'd be best to not put soap directly on her sore spots, so I let her soak for a while.

Whether the girl knew it or not, I wanted her in the best clothes we could find. So, I asked one of the other children to find some of the softest, loveliest clothes from the nursery. After I dried Jan, I covered up her diaper area with cornstarch and her chest with a prescription medicine that we always had for emergencies, thanks to Dr. Clemons. I put on her diaper that Mother Lee had brought to me, then put the outfit on her, and swaddled her in baby blankets. Almost immediately she was at ease with letting everyone else hold her.

She did have a bottle with very ruined milk. Someone washed it and brought it to me with fresh milk and some crackers. She was hungry.

Afterward, we took her to Sunday night service at church. Aunt Ora was the housemother to the younger girls, so Jan went to her department. (To the older girls, she was Aunt Ora. The little girls called her Mama Ora.) Though we had no babies at the time, we had one baby bed. Jan spent the night there. She slept soundly under the careful watch of Aunt Ora. Having never been married, Aunt Ora had no children of her own.

Aunt Ora was a very pretty lady. We questioned her once about not being married. She told us a sad story I wish I could remember about having been in love and what happened to the man.

Early Monday morning, the Welfare Department was called. Only a few hours later, a man came to Childhaven to get as much information as he could about Jan's case. We didn't have many details, but there was one thing we knew for certain. We wanted Jan.

The man told Mother Lee, "It might take a while to run a trace on her so you may keep her until further notice. We will do what we can."

To our surprise, Jan's mother was found. They were able to learn Jan's birthdate and last name. They had her mother sign a letter to terminate her rights.

It was against Childhaven's permit to accept children under the age of two, and for any child to sleep in the same room as an adult. However, the Welfare Department gave permission for Jan to stay, even though she was thirteen months old, and to sleep in Mama Ora's room. Jan adapted to the family and quickly didn't need me anymore. Though Mama Ora loved all the girls, she bonded with Jan in a remarkable way that set their relationship apart. Jan called Aunt Ora simply "Mama."

After graduating from high school, Jan went to the college that many from Childhaven attended—

Freed-Hardeman. She married. They have two children and five grandchildren.

Aunt Ora stayed at Childhaven and kept taking care of her girls until she got too old and a little sick. After she retired from Childhaven, Aunt Ora moved to Tupelo where she lived for twenty-five years. She was involved with Jan's children who thought of Mama Ora as a grandmother. Jan's family spent as much time with Mama Ora as possible.

When Mama Ora could no longer live alone, Jan invited her to live with her and her husband. Mama Ora lived with them for about one year until her death. Jan buried her. Jan said, "I thank God for Childhaven."

"Cast your bread upon the water. After many days it will return to you."
—Ecclesiastes 11:1

Baby Jan (middle) at Childhaven between Chuck Burkeen (L) and Ronnie Haygood (R)

Chapter 20

Johnny, the Arsonist

"You have not lived today until you have done something for someone who can never repay you."
—John Bunyan, Puritan preacher and author of *The Pilgrim's Progress*

I never knew that I could love someone as much as my biological brothers and sister until three brothers entered my life. There were three brothers: Glenn, age seven; Johnny, age five; and baby Pat, age two.

Weeks prior to their arrival at Childhaven, their mother had taken them to an old hotel. After they arrived, a man came by and asked their mother if she wanted to go *somewhere* with him. She told him yes and locked the three children in the hotel room.

Despite her intention to return, the pair went back to the man's house and got drunk for days, leaving the boys unsupervised for an extended period of time. Though they could drink water from the faucet, they had no food to eat.

Being little, bored, curious, and starving, the boys tore apart the room. They found all kinds of things their mother had left behind that they had no business finding: cigarettes, pills, and a box of matches in the bedside drawer. Having seen his mother light cigarettes with the matches, Johnny was intrigued by their glow and power. Simulating the motion he'd seen so many times before, he struck one and set the bed on fire.

The room quickly filled with a big cloud of smoke that went under the door and soon flooded the hallway. Within minutes, other guests discovered the smoke and reported it to the front desk. Soon the three little boys—dirty, hungry, and sick—were rescued. They were picked up by the Welfare Department, then cleaned up and brought to Childhaven.

Mother Lee was distraught by the state the children were in. We tended to them unceasingly. Like all the babies of the house, they took to me easily, and considered me a sister. I'd had a lot of practice with Don and Brenda. I had a sense of how scared they felt, and the type of love they needed.

Because it was summer, my assignment was tending to baby Pat, who had a severe case of scurvy. By permission from the Welfare Department, baby Pat was isolated. I had permission to sleep in the room with him, day and night. He was often sick at night. I was a light sleeper and could hear him and take care of whatever he needed.

I could place my hand on his abdomen and know whether the food would stay down by how much his stomach rumbled. Most of it did not. He could barely even hold down water.

Finally, I decided to feed him small, mashed-up bits of food at little at a time. I would wait a minute or two before giving him additional spoonfuls. I even found some baby food he liked. It took a long time to feed him, but this method did work most of the time, and he slowly began to gain a little weight. Though he was small for his age, he began to round out and was a bright, healthy child. Pretty soon he was beautiful, with bright eyes, a quick wit, and a melodic singing voice. He loved singing almost more than the rest of the house. When he finally started school, he was in the boys' choir at school.

Though all three of the boys were beautiful, Johnny, the middle boy, was by far the most gorgeous. Because he was such a beautiful child, he was sometimes used by local businesses in advertising flyers. Unfortunately, he had a learning delay which put him behind in school.

What he lacked in learning, he compensated for in discipline. He was a rule-follower, kind to everyone he met, and a very loyal friend. He took up for his younger and older brother constantly. What they'd experienced together made them all stronger as they grew. This became important, especially for Johnny, because the spark he ignited in the motel that night was only the first of many fires.

Johnny was the only medically diagnosed arsonist I've ever met. Though his brothers clung to their houseparents, Johnny always found his way into the kitchen, where he'd locate the matches. Childhaven used gas ovens at that time, so there had to be a pilot light for each one, and thus, matches to light them. He became addicted to matches.

He'd confiscate a pack, go outside, find a pile of leaves or a piece of paper, and light up. He always did it outside, but he couldn't control the impulse to ignite the flame. Luckily, it was never anything big. Over time, the adults became more skillful at hiding the matches. But it seemed like the better they were hidden, the more satisfied Johnny would be when he located them.

All the children were in terror and awe of Johnny's obsession, especially because the rest of his personality was completely endearing. He wasn't a bad child. He wasn't a disobedient child. He simply was an arsonist. Throughout the house, everyone began lovingly referring to him as *Johnny the Firebug,* including Mother Lee and Daddy Brock.

At the time, we had a Doberman pinscher named Prince. He had been trained by the military for rescue. He had a track record of saving several of the children from injury or death.

On one blustery fall day, I was outside when I heard several children yelling. I ran to see what was going on and found smoke billowing up from a high circular pile of dry leaves, with Johnny standing in the center. Some of the children were screaming because they were excited. Others screamed because they were afraid. These shouts caught the attention of Prince, who bounded toward the circle.

We all stood back and watched as Prince toppled Johnny over with his big paws, then dragged him out of the pile of blazing leaves. Mother Lee and Daddy Brock were terrified and furious about Johnny's behavior but softened after they learned what had triggered his behavior—despair about a bad grade on his report card.

Fortunately, his fire building decreased. And throughout junior high he was able to make good friends. We certainly grew close. He was tutored (as were all the children who needed it). His grades improved somewhat. My attention to Johnny made him particularly fond of me. His brothers liked me too.

Glenn, the oldest brother, always said of Childhaven, "I wonder how so many beautiful girls all ended up in one place." He went on to graduate high school, marry, and have a large family of his own. He is at all our Childhaven reunions. I love seeing him.

But the middle brother, Johnny, confided in me in a way he didn't with his own brothers, perhaps because I was somewhat of an *older sister* to him.

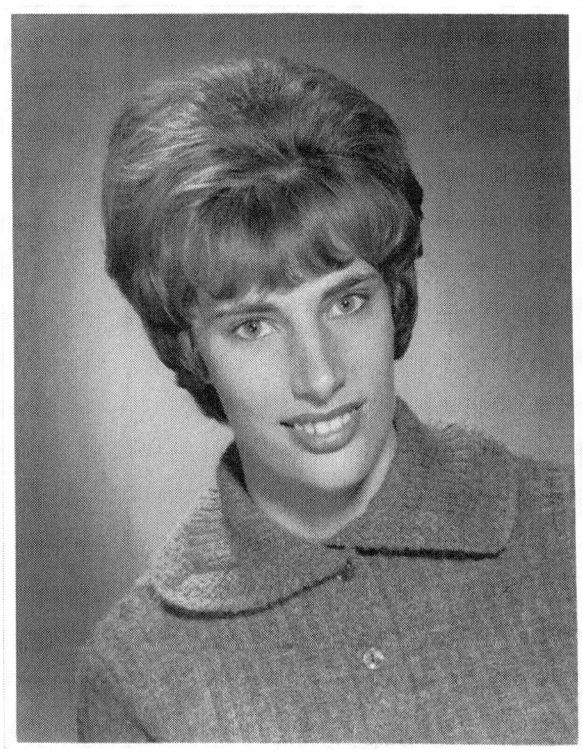

Gail's senior class picture

Chapter 21

College

"Through hard work, perseverance and a faith in God, you can live your dreams."
—Ben Carson

My preparation for college, along with some other children who were old enough to transition out of the home, went smoothly, but I dreaded leaving home. We couldn't come home for three months for fear we wouldn't go back to the new lives we were creating.

My first semester of college at Freed-Hardeman had gone tremendously well. Things were solid, stable, and wonderful. There were unique people there from all walks of life.

Some students had a hard time being away from family but made friends with people that were suite mates. Others weren't sure which clubs to join. They wondered who they would eat meals with. However, I adjusted to the structure of campus life easily because it was similar to Childhaven.

One of my classes was thespians (acting). Then I tried out for and was invited to join the chorus. Between class and my extracurriculars, I was experiencing campus life: enjoying the dorms, going out on Saturday nights, and getting to know boys.

I was on my way to my first thespian meeting when Bill, a boy I had gone on a few dates with, asked if he could walk with me. I agreed. When we got to the auditorium, he became preoccupied with something. That's when Jerrie came to sit by me. We talked and laughed through the whole meeting, as it was a very informal conversation about our next play.

Afterward, Jerrie asked me if he could walk me back to the dorm. I assume Bill thought since he had walked with me to the meeting, he had walking-back-to-the-dorm privileges. So, the three of us walked to my dorm, said *goodnight,* and they went to their dorm.

I certainly liked Jerrie, but I had been dating several boys off and on because I had been determined not to get involved with just one. Jerrie tried to see me more, and he did have a car. In 1963, there were very few cars on campus—maybe twenty boys and one girl had them.

Within a few months, I had gradually stopped going out with all the boys but Jerrie, Bill, and another young man named John.

Because Freed-Hardeman was (and still is) a very conservative Christian college, kissing and holding hands were frowned upon. When I first began exploring things with Bill, we were sitting on a bench outside when he leaned forward and gave me a pretty long kiss. It was broken up with an *ahem*. The dean of students butted in and ordered us to go to his office. In an effort to stay humble, Bill said, "I'm so sorry. Being older, I should have known better."

Then the dean turned to me and asked if I had anything to say. Feeling embarrassed and angry at Bill, I snapped, "Yes, I do have something to say. I am not sorry, and frankly, I enjoyed it."

Both the dean and Bill were surprised, and without much more conversation, we were dismissed.

Outside, Bill asked if we were still on for our evening date. I said, “No way. I don’t go out with boys who apologize for kissing me.”

So, after that, I was down to two, but not really. *What a lucky man Jerrie Barber is* because John was an easy pass for me. I had a hunch John was fond of my suitemates, and I was growing all the more partial to Jerrie, even though he was nineteen and I was twenty-one.

Throughout the fall semester, Jerrie became the boy who would throw a rock at my window instead of spending a dime in the lobby phone to call me to go with him to eat, or whatever he had planned. And soon, he became the young man who would ask me to marry him. Without hesitation, and despite the initial disapproval of Jerrie’s parents, I said *yes*. I don’t think his parents would have liked any girl he would marry at our age, fearing I would take up too much of his time.

Jerrie letting me know it was time to eat in the cafeteria before iPhones.

Suffice it to say, my interests and attention were divided. I had two lives—one at Childhaven and one in college—and both were full of people and lively circumstances to look after. By the time Christmas finals rolled around, I was determined to finish with good grades, but it took a valiant effort. After exams, I returned to Cullman to help out in the office at Childhaven.

A few months later, while the children of Childhaven were happy doing what they did from day to day, I was back in college. One day, one of the men on the board of trustees showed up at Freed-Hardeman. I was sent for. He said, "I just came to tell you Daddy Brock was fired last night."

I was in shock. I knew Childhaven had been doing great in every area I could think of. We were about half self-supporting, which was one of Daddy Brock's goals. However, a majority of the trustees believed it should be *all* church and individual supported, and we children should not be working in our own gardens, milking cows, and raising chickens. The board was worried that if we were able to fully support ourselves, people would quit giving. Daddy Brock did not agree with them.

Many emotions flooded my brain, including anger and sadness, along with questions like, *How stupid can you be? What are the children still there going through, especially Don and Brenda?* It was horrible for me, and I knew it would be for them, both high school seniors at the time. I thought about Johnny, who had been doing so well. I wanted to go home.

A few days later, someone called me and told me the big barn full of hay had caught on fire. This had happened before due to internal combustion in the hay. The fire department thought that was what had happened again, but I thought: *Johnny*.

The trustees were holding a meeting and asked me to come to it, to represent the Childhaven girls. Ronnie, one of the Childhaven boys, attending Harding College in Searcy, Arkansas, was asked to come to the meeting to represent the Childhaven boys. I was not surprised to hear that the older children of Childhaven were extremely upset. The trustees were asking us what they could do to smooth things over. We suggested they repent and hire Daddy Brock back. I pleaded for them to let Mother Lee and Daddy Brock stay, warning the board that they were making a huge mistake.

Sadly, the board's decision was firm. It was challenging to think of all the children who wouldn't be able to learn how to farm, milk the cows, tame the wild bulls, or round up chickens late on a Friday night. We were devastated. Childhaven was never the same.

Daddy Brock and Mother Lee had moved to a house they owned. Ronnie and I went by to visit with them. They were as heartbroken and lost as some of us had been when we came to Childhaven.

After a brief visit, we both went back to our schools and tried to keep up our studies. Then, I got *the call*. The big house was on fire! *Johnny*.

The upper two floors where the fire started were destroyed. Thankfully, they had not yet been converted into living quarters for the children, so no one was there. The fire department made sure all the children were safe. Still, there was water damage.

I talked to Mother Lee and asked her what they had done to Johnny. She didn't know but did know he had done it. I believe one of the longtime employees told the police they needed to talk to Johnny. They did, and he admitted doing it. The police put him in jail, but never locked the door. They would play games with him and bring him food. They thought he would like Cokes, a great treat.

I went home for Spring Break. Someone told me the police were bringing Johnny home to pick up some of his things before they took him to a place for children like him, children with mental issues. He was, I believe, only fourteen years old.

He sent word asking if I would mind coming to see him. He cried in my arms and asked me if I still loved him. I told him I did and that I had always understood him.

The last time I saw Johnny he was looking out the back window of the police car waving at me. The police told me they would continue his education where he was going and that he would have a lot of freedom.

It is a bit confusing as to what happened to the rest of his life, but this is the way it was told to me by various people. Apparently, he did well at the "school." After graduation, he joined the army. After boot camp, he was given some choices as to the department he would like to be a part of. He chose the fire brigade. He said he would like to learn to put out fires instead of setting them.

While still in the army, he stopped on a road to help a woman who was having car trouble. Just as he got back into his car, a tanker truck full of gas hit his truck. It exploded and he was burned to death.

I am praying there is a beautiful man named Johnny in Paradise waiting for Heaven. I know Mother Lee and Daddy Brock would be looking after him. Even there.

Chapter 22

Sarah, the Small One

"One of the most important things you can do on this earth is to let people know they are not alone."
—Shannon L. Alder, inspirational writer and therapist

After freshman year was over, I went home to work in the office until Jerrie and I were married in August. I bonded with several of the newer children at Childhaven. That May, little Sarah came to live with us.

Sarah was an exceptionally beautiful child—petite, with cherub cheeks, and short, thick hair that framed her face. When Sarah arrived at the home, everyone couldn't help but stare at her incredibly handsome father. He was like the movie stars we'd seen on television. We were so *starstruck* by his beauty it took us a moment to realize he was being escorted in by a policeman. Evidently, her father was on his way to prison.

In a final visitation with his four very young children, the entire family grieved. The three older children were desperately clinging to their father and to each other. Sarah, the four-year-old, was sitting some distance away. I couldn't help but think back to the last time I was together with all my siblings and with Daddy after our last picnic, before the social workers took us away to foster care.

Because I worked in the office, I knew a little bit about each of the children's cases and had much more information than the other older children. Apparently, Sarah's father had suspected his wife was having an affair. Following his gut instinct, he left work early on a weekday and found his wife in bed with her lover. Though the children were in the house, he lost his mind, went blind with rage, and ran for his gun. The children followed. That day, they witnessed their father shoot their mother and her lover, then drag their nude, bloody corpses down the stairs and into the front yard.

Before the judge, he pleaded *temporary insanity,* stating, "No one in their right mind would do something so horrific in front of their children." He was charged and sentenced to twenty years in prison. He only served eight. Since he had been a member of the Church of Christ, he knew of Childhaven and asked that his children be brought there.

As a result of the incident, Sarah was terrified of men, even her daddy. She was so traumatized we hardly knew how to help her. I committed to spending as much time with her as possible. She clung to me with all her strength. She needed to hold my hand for hours all day, and because I was tall and thin, I began to have back trouble from leaning to one side to hold her hand. Finally, I managed to get her to hang her tiny fingers from the hip pocket of my jeans.

She cried any time I left the room, and I held back tears any time I disappointed her. Her attachment to me became so strong that she'd weep until she got sick at night if I couldn't be there to care for her. She was happy sitting in a little chair next to me in the office as I did my job.

Irrational triggers would pop up everywhere for her. We assumed everything took her back to the moment she witnessed the murder of her mother. A sound. A smell. To cope, she would hold her breath until she passed out. Even worse, she would bite her arm until blood dripped to the floor. It was as if inflicting pain on herself gave her a sense of control.

Finally, under her doctor's instructions, Sarah was allowed to live in my room. The rules normally forbade any two children sleeping in the same bed or a young child sleeping in the same room as an older child, but because I was of age and could properly care for her, they let her stay. Eventually, after weeks of distress, Sarah was able to get consistent sleep and moved back to the nursery.

Mealtime was exceptionally bad for Sarah because that's when boys and men were around. She was also afraid of the sensory overload of the dining room. Almost from the time of her arrival, I had eaten with her in the kitchen. But after she had been there several weeks, I thought it was best to ease her into eating with the other children. I prepared her a space during her first meal, a chair just inside the door. Our goal was to ease a little closer to the dining table each day, until finally, we made it.

We were inseparable. I could hardly shower or go to the bathroom without her interrupting me. In more ways than I had bargained for, I had become Sarah's caretaker. Though I was devoted to Childhaven, this became a bit much for me, because I had a long-distance fiancé, and I was planning a wedding.

Additionally, I'd promised to take off for one week, to teach vacation Bible school in Jerrie's hometown before I left Childhaven for good. We were puzzled, not sure what to do with Sarah. When I initially told her I had to leave, she panicked. She cried until she was dry heaving and covered with mucus. I approached the new superintendent and got permission to take her with me. I was grateful to Jerrie's parents for letting us stay with them in such strange circumstances.

Houseparent Aunt Ora and I were concerned about our trip, since the only way to get to Columbia, Tennessee, was by Greyhound bus. Given Sarah's fear of men, I could only imagine how traveling would go. Thankfully, when we arrived at the bus station in Cullman, Sarah was sound asleep. With her head propped up on my shoulder, I looked for seats on an aisle where there were no men in sight. I found an empty space only two rows from the front. The bus was not packed but it was still full enough to make me nervous.

I thought we were in the clear until we began to pull away from the bus stop. The sound of the door closing woke Sarah, and in the distance, she saw a tall, young, Black man making his way to our seat. She immediately burst into tears and screams and tried to bite her arm. I was able to prevent her from drawing blood.

The man made eye contact with me and said, "I'll move. I didn't mean to scare her."

Caught off guard, I responded, "No. She saw a man murder her mother. I promise, she is afraid of all men."

He graciously said, "I'll move. I'll find somewhere else to sit." And he did. I was embarrassed, but I was grateful and mouthed *thank you* to him. People around were being nice and a few cried on Sarah's behalf. Finally, I got her calm again.

By the time we got to Columbia, Sarah had gone back to sleep. I was tremendously relieved. I knew Jerrie was picking me up in his pickup truck. I was worried there wouldn't be enough space for all of us, and Sarah and I might have to ride in the truck bed. I managed to get into the truck without waking her. When we got to his parent's house, Mrs. Barber had set up Jerrie's baby bed for her. To make sure she settled in soundly, I lay with her on my bed until she felt comfortable resting.

Soon after, I went to Jerrie's room across the hall, in earshot of Sarah. Jerrie and I began roughhousing, playfighting and wrestling, making more of a commotion than I'd realized. We'd assumed Sarah was asleep until she burst through the door and plowed into Jerrie like a mini steamroller, kicking and hitting him. I had to pull her off him and drag her screaming into the guest room. I closed the door and explained to her that we were playing, and that I was safe.

For the rest of the week, Sarah was fearful of Jerrie and his father. We could not be in the same room together. Not even at mealtime. Jerrie and his parents would eat, then Sarah and I would eat.

Every night, I put her to bed, thinking she was asleep. Then I'd go visit Jerrie next door. Inevitably, she was always pretending to be asleep, and was on high alert. We figured our best response was to *show* her that Jerrie was safe.

The next night, when I knew Sarah was still pretending to be asleep, I went to Jerrie and told him to follow my lead. I led him into the hall until we stood just outside her door so she could see and hear us. We kissed and I told Jerrie I loved him.

She didn't move.

He said he loved me and would never hurt me or let anyone else hurt me because he loved me. He then said his daddy would never hurt me, and they would love and play with Sarah if she would let them. We talked some more and held hands while she was doing her best to keep her eyes closed. Then, we left her to see what would become of it.

The next morning, Sarah surprisingly slept in, so I ate breakfast with the family. Finally, we heard her bound down the hall with a newfound sense of warmth toward her surroundings. She approached Jerrie and said, "Why don't me and you get into your car, and you take me to the store and buy me a little red truck to play with?"

We all looked at each other with amusement and laughed. It had worked!

"We'll do that right after we eat." Jerrie asked, "Will you eat with us?" Sarah nodded and had her first peaceful meal with men sitting at the table.

After breakfast, Jerrie kept his word. He took Sarah to town and bought her a little red truck. When they returned, his dad was mowing grass.

"I think I'll just walk with him for a while," she said, pointing to Jerrie's father. Though he had just started mowing, Sarah followed him every step of the way. It was evident—her recovery had begun.

Over the next few weeks back at Childhaven, I gradually moved Sarah out of my room, allowing her to stay every other night. She began to need me less and less and started feeling safer with the other children. By early August, she was back in the nursery.

Sarah would frequently ask me about Jerrie because she absolutely adored him. Given the way that he and his parents had accommodated my circumstances and one of our own at Childhaven, I fell more in love with him throughout the summer.

Though we had been engaged for only a short period of time, the quality of our relationship ran deep. I figured this was exactly the way it should be, and even though Jerrie had never met Mama and

Daddy, he had the blessing of Mother Lee and Daddy Brock, and that felt sacred in a way that was inexplicable. Later, he met Daddy, Wayne, Frances, and her children.

Because of the blessings of Childhaven, I was able to experience a life built on safety, family, and happiness. In turn, I began dreaming of how I would take those concepts out into the world and make them my own.

Childhaven in 2014

Chapter 23

The Mitchells

"Train up a child in the way he should go and when he is old, he will not depart from it."
—Proverbs 22:6

Every child who arrived at Childhaven was given a sponsor—usually a church—to ensure they were properly supported throughout every season of their stay. Brenda and I were sponsored by the Tuscumbia Church of Christ on 4th street in Tuscumbia, Alabama. Every year we eagerly anticipated the clothing they supplied us: one set in spring and one in winter. Donald was sponsored by a church in Mobile, Alabama.

Christmas supplies and decorations were supplied by the sponsors and also businesses from various parts of Alabama.

Occasionally, the children would visit the churches to become acquainted with the congregation. Certain members of the community would visit Childhaven to provide each child with a sense of belonging.

Our sponsors visited Brenda and me often. They always did more than expected. Individuals would sometimes surprise us with a pretty sweater or a little money. And more importantly, visits.

The first time I met the sponsor congregation was a bright summer day in 1953. I was ten. Brenda was seven. We'd come with our choral group to sing for the church on Sunday afternoon after the congregation's picnic. After our performance, we'd eat under the pavilion, play on the playground, then go to stay with one of the families.

Most of the time we stayed with the *Mitchells*—we called the wife "Mrs. Mitchell" and the husband "Ralph." On our first visit with them, Mrs. Mitchell gave Brenda and me each our own tiny purse—both had ten one-dollar bills tucked away in the pocket. I had never had that much money at one time before. I wondered how any person could ever spend that much. I felt so extravagant. We were very excited to be rich!

They took us home with them to a large piece of land where they had lived for most of their married life and raised all their children. Their house was picturesque: big and white, with navy shutters that perfectly framed the windows. Ralph still worked. Mrs. Mitchell had a ceramic shop on the property next to their house. Brenda preferred being outside playing with their grandchildren who lived ncxt door.

I was a creative child, so walking into Mrs. Mitchell's shop always fascinated and inspired me. The first time I visited, she gave me an apron of my very own, and carved out a cool, gray slab of clay for molding. She filled a bucket with water and dipped a sponge in it, guiding me through the process of making a handmade rose. The longer I worked on the shape of my small project, the more I fell in love with the feeling of slimy wet clay against my fingers. Then she taught me how to paint pots.

The pots, vases, and figures were poured in molds. Then cleaned up, smoothed, and painted before firing. Mrs. Mitchell taught me about how the colors would look after they were baked—pearlescent lavender, misty pink, and iridescent blue. I couldn't get enough of making art. Mrs. Mitchell and I were kindred spirits in that way. She encouraged me to use as many materials as I wanted, and to sculpt to my heart's content.

Because it was important for us to get to know the rest of the church, we were often pulled in several social directions during our visits. While Brenda and I were satisfied to spend time with other families, we were always pleased to return to the Mitchells.

Every time we made our way up their long driveway, it felt more like home. They had a big dog outside hooked to a chain. Brenda and I would try to outrun her, knowing she could only go so far.

The Mitchells were strict with us about meals. If we went out to eat and didn't eat all our food, they would take our food home. Then for our next meal, we ate those leftovers while they ate fresh food. This only happened twice. We were okay with this, because they were structured in all the right places, and flexible in every other area.

One of our favorite occasions with the Mitchells was a shower we had early on, hosted by the ladies of the church at a home belonging to a younger couple in the church. We gathered in a large, cozy kitchen with a full potluck meal prepared: delicious cheesy casseroles, finger foods, and freshly baked pies. The home was decorated with streamers and brightly colored balloons.

After several hours of socializing, Brenda and I sat in a chair in front of everyone and opened gifts (which were mostly unnecessary things like jewelry, candy, and clothing). We felt honored and proud to take home items and show them to the other girls.

What we thought was a one-time event occurred several times. Once I was shocked by a huge box of Kotex. I had seen the older girls with these boxes but had no idea what they were for. I was ten years old.

When we spent holidays with the Mitchells we were treated like royalty. We lost track of time until Mrs. Mitchell would tuck us in every night, where we would savor every good sleep until the day we returned to Childhaven.

We enjoyed our long weekends away getting to know different members of the church. Church was especially wonderful. Teachers and students were amazed at our Bible knowledge. On one memorable visit, my Sunday School teacher decided to have a "Where Is It in the Bible?" contest.

She would read certain verses. It was our job to verbally cite where each one could be found. Some were identifiable, others were a little more obscure. The class was made up of all girls. The teacher divided us in two groups. A few of the girls were more eager to answer than others. I was particularly excited because I knew most of the verses, and my hand would often shoot up in the air. One girl on the other team was very bright. Right before the bell, the score was tied.

Just before being given a verse, I opened my Bible to Isaiah—looking for something to break the tie. I was surprised when my eyes landed on the exact verse our teacher had just read—a scripture I'd never heard. Excitedly, I called out the answer and our team won. It was such a neat experience that helped Brenda and me bond with the other children.

For years, the teen girls' Sunday School class had always taken up money to buy our school lunches. We had been just *the orphans* who took a portion of their money. But that was the day we became their *friends*. Suddenly, I was a person to them and not just a project. They shifted to treating us like well-dressed, smart children, who just happened to live at Childhaven, due to difficult circumstances.

Over the thirteen years I lived at Childhaven, our sponsoring church saw us through the best and worst of times. The Mitchells practically raised us, counseling Brenda and me through our school years, matters of grief, and *boy troubles.*

Mrs. Mitchell and Gail in her pottery studio
(from a local newspaper)

Chapter 24

The Early Years of Marriage

"There is no more lovely, friendly, and charming relationship, communion or company than a good marriage."
—Martin Luther

When I married Jerrie on August 18, 1964, Mrs. Mitchell was as thrilled as Mama would have been. She fully approved of the man who had integrated himself into my life at Childhaven, and who loved me so much. The church offered us the building to have the wedding. So we decided to marry there.

The Mitchells were honored to serve as stand-in parents for the wedding. They did all they could to make it a beautiful wedding, as did the rest of the congregation. A year earlier, they had made a trip to Spain. While there, Mrs. Mitchell bought me a Spanish wedding vail she thought I might need soon.

One of the families paid to have my dress and my bridesmaids' dresses made. Another decorated the church for the reception and threw me an all-day shower that lasted from ten in the morning to sundown. In addition to their contributions, a quartet offered to sing at our wedding.

Close to three hundred people attended—all members of that church and sister churches who knew me from being a Childhaven child. There were even other people from around the area who came, who didn't even go to the church that sponsored me. I was amazed to see how many families came. There were all kinds of people there, including missionaries from several countries.

They pooled their resources to give me gifts that they placed on a long table in the foyer. The mountainous pile almost touched the ceiling by the end of the shower. I received several sets of china and crystal, can openers, toasters, blenders, silverware, glasses, and more aprons than I could keep track of.

There were *hundreds* of presents. My Sunday School class gave me my flatware, and several things I could use right away. I received fifty-two sets of sheets and pillowcases, which inevitably later became my wedding gifts to other people because I didn't have to go out and spend money. I couldn't help but laugh at the irony of having, no sheets as a little child, to having enough for a small village. To this day, I still have one of those original sets of sheets packed in cellophane that I never have opened, just because I don't need to, and I don't want to. It is in my hall closet.

One of the strangest gifts I received was also one of the most valuable: I believe the same woman who had bought me a box of Kotex as a ten-year-old bought me huge boxes with the intention of saving me money in the long term. Though I had no idea where I could store them all—I *oohed and ahhed* along with every other girl in the room who understood the hassle of stocking up for *lady troubles* every month.

The friends I'd made in Sunday School kept a detailed book of the names and addresses of the gift givers for me. They even supplied the fancy stationery and stamps. I made out 165 thank-you cards in the days following my reception.

It was the beginning of a long-standing friendship, and a parental love that complemented my relationship with Mother Lee and Daddy Brock.

Daddy Brock married us. As I stood at the altar with Jerrie and said *I do,* I glanced out at the many parents I inherited over the years who had always desired the best in life for me. I couldn't wait to embark upon my new life with Jerrie and exceed their expectations.

Wedding announcement in the newspaper.

My marriage to Jerrie began on a shoestring budget, but we've always said that what we lacked in means we made up for in devotion to each other. In the beginning, Jerrie was making sixty-five dollars per month by preaching for four congregations. One paid fifteen dollars for every Sunday service. The others paid a little closer to twenty dollars. By the grace of God, we were able to attend school, pay rent, buy groceries, and give to the church. We were spread thin on all resources, but most of all, time. Many wanted Jerrie to preach for them.

The Sunday before our wedding, Jerrie was called to a church in Corinth, Mississippi, about thirty miles away from Freed-Hardeman. They said, "We want Jerrie to teach Sunday morning Bible class, preach for us on Sunday morning and Sunday night, and teach on Wednesday nights." Graciously, they offered Jerrie seventy-five dollars a week, which was more money than either of us had ever made.

And of course, *we were happy to do it,* not just because of the money, but because we wanted to heed God's call in our lives. That Sunday morning as an almost-married couple, I drove while Jerrie used the time to rehearse his sermon.

We felt a heavy conviction in our hearts to serve where we were needed. Though it was cumbersome at times, being available to these communities was our joy. We had to make time where there was none, which was the top adjustment of *many* we made during that season.

Early in our marriage, Jerrie and I found out we were opposite in many smaller things. Where I'm more emotional, empathic, and creative, Jerrie is structured, logical, and resolute. But we were lucky to find we aligned on the major things: church, family, and money.

From the beginning, we were both frugal. It mades sense, given my childhood. We scraped by and saved $200 during our first year of marriage. This was *a lot* for the time—especially considering his salary. To this day, we still have our budget books from when Jerrie made one hundred dollars per week. Our ten dollars allotted for groceries was all planned out. We'd sit down each week with spiral notebooks and a calculator to review our bank balances. Though everything is automatic now, it's something we still practice. We budget together. We set ourselves up for success early, worked hard, and saw it pay off. This laid the foundation for disciplines we would practice the rest of our lives together.

Our wedding on August 18, 1964

For better and for worse, the church always came first for us. We planned our wedding day around it and planted our marriage inside of it. This has been difficult at times, but it has ultimately been our life's greatest reward.

With $150 in traveler's checks, we got married on a Tuesday, August 18, 1964—certainly not one of the most popular days of the week to get married. We did this because we were scheduled to have a rehearsal on Monday before the ceremony. Because we were in Corinth for Jerrie's preaching, we had to make sure to be back home by the following Sunday, so we only had from Tuesday night through Saturday evening for a honeymoon.

The only thing between Alabama and our Smoky Mountain destination was Chattanooga, Tennessee. So, we went to Rock City and then drove up through the Smokies. Jerrie took my hand as we ran to the top of Clingmans Dome, the highest point in the Smoky Mountains. Once we got to the top, we were inside of a cloud. Breathing the mist of the cloud felt very good to our lungs (but was not too good for the hair).

Jerrie and I then went to Gatlinburg, Tennessee as well, as he was already familiar with it. Out of our $150 budget for the honeymoon, we still had a *whole* ten dollars to enjoy once we got back home.

The trip itself was wonderful. We cruised through the rolling, plush hills of Tennessee in Jerrie's light blue 1961 Ford Falcon. I'd roll the windows down and let the wind whip through my hair. We'd listen to the song of the squeaking clutch that could never be fixed, no matter how many times we took it in. We greased it. Oiled it. But it always got around us. Over time it became a mark of pride that it made anyone in the passenger seat wince. Something about the quirkiness made the car more endearing.

When we got home, reality set back in, and days filled quickly each week. It left little time for bonding. We were lonely for each other. Still, we made it through the grueling years of college, which transitioned into the years of family planning.

The church at Corinth gave us a party and some wedding gifts when we got home from our honeymoon. They gave us a wonderful five-quart wooden bucket ice cream freezer and an electric blanket. It was hot so we turned up the air conditioner and slept under it the first night.

After the wedding, Jerrie and I settled nicely into a little house right off the college campus, on a little street called Teacher Row. We were very much integrated into the education community, as every neighbor we had was an educator. We received a very warm welcome, namely because I was so good with children and always offered my babysitting services if someone was in need. Our neighbors on the right and left had four children each. When I'd watch them, their preferred place was our house. Sometimes, both families would need a sitter at the same time. Jerrie would leave the house for class, and I would stay behind with eight children of different ages tugging at my hands, asking me for snacks, begging me to play.

One day, while managing the entire bunch, a salesman came to our door selling his wares. I'm sure he heard me groan at the sound of the doorbell before greeting him with an overwhelmed expression and a group of tiny children yelling at the top of their lungs. My eyes met his. He smiled and abruptly said, "Never mind." Then, he turned on his heels and left. I guess he thought if I had that many children, I couldn't afford whatever he was peddling. I certainly appreciated him being able to read the moment.

Regarding our finances, we were doing okay. An anonymous family had paid for my education. Jerrie's family had paid for his. This was a tremendous blessing because we were able to use the funds we made outside of class to sustain our modest lifestyle. Jerrie was preaching on Sundays. The congregation took great care of us giving us their garden produce and taking us out for meals.

While we struggled with all the common issues of being newlyweds, we were quite happy. Our spiritual community helped us temper challenging times. They supported us through the birth of our two children and lavished them with as much care as Brenda, Don, and I had received during our years at Childhaven.

Chapter 25

Motherhood

"When you have faith in God,
you don't have to worry about the future.
You just know it's all in His hands.
You just go to and do your best."
—Elder Bryan Mathison, author of "Faith in Prayer"

Being good with children and wildly in love with Jerrie, I was excited to be a mother, despite the fears that all pregnant women face. Appreciating the blessing of pregnancy got me through some of the most difficult days of carrying my children.

After four years of marriage, my first pregnancy with our son, Jerrie Wayne, was so easy that it was a tad misleading. I felt good with him. Energetic even.

His birth on August 31, 1968, was perfect, even though he weighed over eight pounds. When Jerrie Wayne was born, his eyes were pools of blue like nothing I'd ever seen. They looked like the whole sky gazing down on a lake, and his smile was the glistening sun.

Back then, we lived in a tiny community of two hundred, but there were little towns all around. When we had a baby shower, we got everything we needed. I got so many baby clothes Jerrie Wayne only wore some of them once.

Jerrie's mother gave me his stroller, highchair, and baby crib she still had in the attic. We've used that baby crib in our family all the way down to our grandchildren. It's in the attic if I need it for a great-grand.

My pregnancy with Christi three years later was anything but easy. Before I knew I was pregnant, I had begun to swell in my hands, feet, and face. Soon after, I began itching a lot and it was getting worse. I endured it as long as I could before going to an allergist.

He informed me that my allergy was one of those nine-month kinds. He did a pregnancy test and pronounced me pregnant with a girl, as only girls cause this kind of allergy. After examining my eyes, he said my symptoms were temporary and should only last through my pregnancy. He had only seen one other case of this. So, I suffered for months on four Benadryl a day, developing dozens of skin tags on my chest and arms, confused as to how I could be allergic to my baby. We named her Christi Gail.

The sickness got so bad that at one point my gynecologist suggested abortion. He observed that Christi was essentially poisoning me. He knew that she would be a sick baby. But I was horrified at the suggestion.

"Absolutely not," I insisted. "I can deal with a sick child," I said. My childhood had demonstrated that I was a survivor. I already loved my unborn baby enough to fight for her. My doctor informed me that ironically the only similar condition he'd seen was in another patient that was also a member of the Church of Christ. He noted that my condition looked like I had chicken pox, but hers looked more like she had smallpox. She had been permanently scarred from it.

Coincidentally, only a short time later, Jerrie was preaching at a gospel meeting—what other churches would refer to as a *revival*—when a family invited us over for supper. The wife commented on my pregnancy and said she'd had her baby in Madisonville. As she spoke, I noticed what looked like smallpox scars on her face and arms. Casually, I asked if Dr. Stanley had been her gynecologist.

"Yes. And I had this horrible allergy during my pregnancy," she began.

As she told me her horrible story, I knew this was the other woman my doctor had spoken about. I found her perseverance encouraging. I figured it was confirmation from the Lord that *I would be okay.*

When I first realized I was pregnant with Christi, I wondered whose eyes she would have. When I held Christi in my arms for the first time on August 8, 1971, and saw those beautiful eyes gazing up at me, I knew I had made the right decision in going through with the pregnancy. However, her early days of life were bleak. She was born weak and sickly. Her doctors told me she would never be able to live alone.

Despite not having much energy, she seemed entirely normal to me. We saw the doctor often and that kept tabs on her depressed immune system. She fell ill easily. She would run a high fever with the slightest infection.

Throughout early childhood, she was in and out of school with illnesses. Twice she was in the hospital with a 107-degree temperature. To reduce her fever, physicians had to poison her with the same frog poison that people put on arrows. Both times she slept around sixty to seventy hours, as our friends and family prayed unceasingly for her health.

The medical staff promised her body would cool down. *It had to*. If it didn't, the fever would kill her. Luckily, it broke every time. I attributed this to God's mercies and answered prayers.

Her teachers always welcomed her back heartily. Christi was an outstanding student who loved learning. She did well so long as the school secretary kept a thermometer handy for her.

Christi always bounced back, even from the worst of illnesses. On one occasion when she was seven, we had been to West Kentucky for a gospel meeting and learned afterward that some of the congregation had scarlet fever. When we first got home, all was well. But then, Christi boarded the school bus. Within an hour she'd gone to the office where they took her temperature, then called me. It was 103 degrees. I called her doctor to let him know we were on our way.

By that point, we'd built a relationship with him. We never had to wait. When we arrived, her temperature was 105 degrees. We were sent home for fear that if she were admitted to the hospital, she might catch something else and not survive. I had been told many times before that she might not survive, but I never believed it.

On a couple of occasions when she was sick, I would think one thing, her doctor another. I was always right. This time he asked me, "What do you think it is?"

I said, "Scarlet fever." He agreed. It was.

This time Christi's doctor was so concerned he called two retired physicians to help him. Church ladies were a great help by sitting with her and bringing food. Even nurses volunteered to come to the house to stay with her for a few hours so I could sleep. Doctors noted the only thing that would keep her alive was two adult aspirin every four hours and two adult Tylenol every four hours in between.

Back then, we didn't know about Reye's syndrome. It is a rapidly progressive brain disease, primarily seen in children, that can be triggered by taking aspirin to treat viral infections such as chicken pox or, in her case, scarlet fever. This is why today it's not recommended to give children aspirin.

Every Monday, I would take her to the doctors for more tests. Their routine became our routine. As a result, Christi fell eight weeks behind in school. Throughout that season, I prayed a lot. I begged God to make her well. I asked that He give her to me whole and not sicker than before.

By week eight, they said they wanted to see me in the office.

My heart dropped at the thought that she might not make it. One doctor ushered me in and invited me to *sit down*. He was tall but bent from doing so much surgery. Another doctor told me they did not want to get my hopes up. But as of today, her body chemistry is perfectly balanced.

Before Christi was released from her doctor's care, her doctor stopped me. He said, "All the praying didn't hurt." They didn't really know why but thought the scarlet fever and the extreme temperature might have shocked her body, like using a defibrillator to shock a person's heart.

Christi's return to school after the long sickness

When I took her back to school on Monday, teachers, office staff, and students were excited to see her. Her teacher said, "This is wonderful! Today is picture day." She had not had her hair washed in eight weeks. This picture is beautiful. One of my favorites of her.

Today, her body chemistry is perfect. If that's not an answered prayer, I don't know what is.

Chapter 26

Seeing the World

"The greatest legacy one can pass on to one's children and grandchildren is not money or other material things accumulated in one's life, but rather a legacy of character and faith."

—Billy Graham

A dear friend we met when Jerrie Wayne was a baby had three girls. He worked hard and never took off for vacation. He was saving for a wonderful trip when he retired. He died suddenly and they never got that wonderful trip. No memories. No pictures. No tales to tell their children. Because of him we learned to do special things with special people when we could.

One of the wonderful things about rearing our children were vacations. Jerrie Wayne was nineteen months old when we started going to Gatlinburg, TN as a family. It was winter. I have a beautiful picture of him playing in the snow. Every year until Jerrie Wayne started school, we would go on vacation in different seasons. For years, we stayed at Watson's Motel.

Back then, Gatlinburg was much smaller than it is now. We liked going to the nearby town of Pigeon Forge where there was only the old mill (no restaurants), and Hill-Billy Village, where one could buy many inexpensive trinkets. That was all of Pigeon Forge.

When Jerrie Wayne was two and a half and I was pregnant with Christi, we decided to climb Mount Le Conte and spend the night. Jerrie Wayne was a very overactive boy who loved the outdoors. On this occasion, he was a bit fretful and wanted to be carried part of the time. On the way back the next day and even in the car he wanted to be held and was crying a little. Then, I noticed he had a fever. I guess he knew there was something wrong but didn't know what to do.

Through tears, he said, "We've been up here a whole week and now we're going home, and I haven't even seen a mountain, Mama" (a nod to John Denver's song, "Take Me Home, Country Roads"). We'd been in the mountains for a week. When we got home and to the doctor, we learned he had an ear infection.

Jerrie Wayne in the mountains in the snow

Christi was a very easygoing child, content in most situations. She was four when we stayed a few days in Cherokee, North Carolina, instead of Gatlinburg, so we could go see *Unto These Hills,* an outdoor play that tells the story of the Native Americans being driven from their homeland and the Trail of Tears.

While we were at the play, Jerrie Wayne was misbehaving badly. Jerrie asked him several times, "Do you need an adjustment?" We called spankings "adjustments," kind of like a secret code. "Do you need an adjustment?" usually got the job done. If not, there was a trip to the restroom. Spankings were never given in public.

His behavior became worse, even brat-like. Jerrie finally asked him why he was being so bad.

He said, "There isn't a bathroom in this whole place!"

Jerrie said, "There are some there and there and there," pointing to the restrooms nearby.

So, Jerrie Wayne sat down and was a perfect boy the rest of the play.

On Sunday, we were going to church where Native Americans and others, especially vacationers, went. Christi was very clingy on the way until she finally started crying. Thinking she was sick, I asked what was wrong. Sobbing by now, she said, "I don't want to go to church with naked people." (Some of the Native Americans in the play had very little clothing on.) She was a happy girl to be told otherwise.

Several years later, we went to see the play again. Jerrie Wayne, five or six at the time, asked me, "Where is their color television?" (Ours was black-and-white.)

I said, "Darling, they didn't have TV then."

He said, "They did last time."

There was no way to talk him out of it. I guess he had dreamed it so real that he thought it so. It didn't do any harm for him to think it.

Jerrie and I went to Israel in 1973, leaving our two- and five-year-olds with an aunt and uncle. The trip was one of the highlights of our lives. We took many slide photographs of our trip.

When Jerrie Wayne was in middle school, I was at the school a lot. I was president of the PTA and did volunteer and substitute teaching. They were studying Israel in Jerrie Wayne's class. He told his teacher about the slides we had. His teacher asked me if I would show the slides to the class. I said I would only show them if I could tell the students why I had made the pictures. I told her that I would say God and Jesus a lot. It was fine with her.

The next time she saw me, she told me a lot of the teachers wanted their students to see my slides. So, once a week for six weeks, I spoke in the auditorium about the Bible, God, and Jesus, to about two hundred students. They loved it.

Because they all knew me, many would hug me and thank me afterward. One girl came up to me and said, “I’ve gone to Sunday School all my life and I have learned more from you than all of that.”

When Jerrie Wayne and Christi became old enough for school, we went on vacation only in the summer. One of our favorite things to do was go to Cades Cove. At that time, people still lived there. In the 1920s, the government started purchasing Cades Cove land for part of the formation of the Smoky Mountains National Park. Many people sold their land and left, but people were also allowed to stay until they died with “life leases” for less money, and limitations on hunting and trapping.

We always bought honey from one man. He told us one day, "You would be surprised how many people steal it." He would sometimes hide in a beehive-type box and watch someone steal his honey and go to their car. He would get the license plate number and another person would stop them as they left the one-way circle road and either retrieve the honey or make them pay. At night, the entrance gate was locked. Even residents couldn't come and go.

The school bus driver who picked up the children also unlocked the gate to the entrance to the road. That time of the morning, there were many deer, bears, and turkeys just getting out to eat. We would be waiting for him to show up to be the first to go around the road. We loved looking for and counting the various animals and talking to the people who were just getting out with their various things to sell.

Later, the grandchildren loved this same adventure. We have great-grandchildren now. The adventure is still the same for them, although the people are gone. Cades Cove, Gatlinburg, and especially Pigeon Forge have changed greatly, but only we know that. We let them enjoy it as it is.

Family portrait in the summer of 1976

We went to the Smoky Mountains for years as a family. One of the most beautiful outdoor scenes I have seen happened on one of our fall vacations. The trees were in full color and then it snowed. The snow was on the leaves of the trees, and the leaves encircled the snow on the ground. God is good to allow us to see such beauty.

Before our children were born, we decided to climb the Chimney Tops. We were strong and had often climbed mountains. Jerrie's parents were with us. We climbed the first part easily. Then, we came to a sign that said, "For experienced hikers only." Thinking we were experienced, we continued. Then, it started to rain. The ground was clay. I think everyone fell at least once but me. We were wet, muddy, and exhausted when we got to the bottom. But now we can always say, "We climbed the Chimney Tops." Years later, Jerrie, Jerrie Wayne, and our son-in-law, Brian, climbed them again. The Chimney Tops burned but were not destroyed in the Gatlinburg fires in 2016.

We took at least one other vacation every year. When the children were older, they took turns choosing where they wanted to go every other year. One of our favorite places was Mammoth Cave and the Cave City area. We would stay at the Wigwam Village, which were motel rooms in the shape of wigwams.

One year, we took the six-hour dinner tour in Mammoth Cave. (I don't think they do that anymore). I was so proud of our two children. All the other children were complaining about being tired. Some, even ten-year-olds, were begging their daddies to carry them. I thought, *get your children playing outside, and they won't be so weak*. We had read some information by Dr. James Dobson (a popular psychologist at the time) about taking your preadolescent child on a trip just before they entered middle school. Dr. Dobson had workbooks and tapes we could purchase. The idea was for dads to take sons and moms to take daughters.

Jerrie Wayne was first. He chose Mammoth Cave and the Wigwams. He knew basically what the tapes were about and confided in me that he would enjoy the trip but already knew all about what he thought would be on the tapes. When they got home, he ran to me, hugged me, and whispered, "I learned a few things."

Christi also chose the same place when it was our turn three years later. We ate a wonderful breakfast every morning at "Christy's." The preparing for adolescence CDs and workbook package was a most excellent idea from Dr. Dobson.

Wigwam Village where we took our children on their pre-adolescent trip

We went to Israel again in 1993. Jerrie and I were both in excellent health and could handle the trip and all activities with ease.

That year we had a very small group of twenty-two travelers. We had a large van with a driver named Alone, and a guide whose nickname was Leo. Somehow, we built a quick friendship with Leo.

At the Sea of Galilee, when it was time to disembark, Leo told our group to be the last to get off. After everyone else had gotten off, he told us to stay.

The captain and crew were friends. Leo had asked him to take us back out and further than the regular cruise. I had brought some canvases and paint. I painted a painting of the shoreline for each of them. They were thankful and thought it was wonderful. When we left, they gave each of the ladies a long-stemmed rose. Leo gave me an over two-thousand-year-old coin he had purchased while some of us were eating.

When Leo was visiting the states for three months to teach at a university, he called me. He used his real name, which was about twenty letters long. I didn't recognize it at all. Finally, he said, "It's Leo." I felt very honored he would remember me and still have my phone number. The main thing he wanted me to know was how much he liked being our guide. He and his wife had been separated for some reason when we were in Israel. He said, "I know this will make you happy: my wife and I have reconciled."

We were to go again to Israel in 1996, but at that time Christi and her husband Brian were expecting a baby at the same time. I didn't go, but Jerrie did.

We had always hoped our children would go sometime. In 2018, Jerrie's mother died. She left enough money for us to take all the family that wanted to go. Jerrie and I, both of our children, their spouses, and three of the six grandchildren went. The best part of the trip was seeing their faces as they saw the biblical places we had seen forty-five years earlier.

For us and now them, the Sea of Galilee is special. They haven't built a church building over it yet. Most historical places do have a church over them. That's good and bad. Good because it protects the place. Bad because it is not in its natural setting. We do look forward to the Dead Sea and the Jordan River also.

Israel holds a special place in our memory files. Jerrie and I have plans to go back in 2025. I'll be eighty-two. Jerrie will be eighty. Jerrie is in most excellent health. I am not. When Jerrie goes back to Israel, Jackson, our oldest great-grand, will be twelve. I hope he wants to go.

The children, grandchildren, and one great-grandchild have plans to return. They can hardly wait.

Family in Israel January 2019: Wyatt Houston, Jerrie Wayne, Terri Barber; Jerrie and Gail Barber; Brian, Christi, Brittan, Braden Parsons

We decided that if it was a good idea for our children to go on a trip just before they entered middle school, we might enjoy the same kind of trips with the grandchildren but without the tapes and books. Our granddaughter Elizabeth was nine when, on our family vacation, we told everyone of our plan. If we were physically and financially able, we would like to take each grandchild on a private vacation with us for four or five days.

All were excited and began to tell where they would like to go. When it came Elizabeth's time, she chose Jerusalem. Jerrie said, "How about within three hundred miles of Nashville?" She chose Mammoth Cave and the Wigwams. She had never been there but had seen pictures and had heard her dad and Christi talk about it. We gave her a hundred dollars to spend. Half had to be spent on other people.

The next four grandchildren went to Gatlinburg. There was an exhibit at the time called Christus Gardens, "The Life of Christ in Wax." Next to that was a hundred-year-old house. It all belonged to the parents of a good friend. Once, we got to stay in the house. We had hoped to again, but they had torn it down.

The youngest wanted to go to Memphis to see Elvis Presley's house, Graceland, then a Redbirds' (minor league baseball) game, and the zoo.

I have several pictures of the grandchildren climbing a rock on Clingmans Dome. When we got pictures back, I noticed a sign, "Do not climb on these rocks." Every year, we take a day to go on a picnic and play in a creek, one of our most fun days. We started this with our own children, then did it with the grandchildren, and now we're doing it with great-grandchildren.

We stayed in motels at first. Over the years, we went from renting a small cabin to a large one, then a much larger one. This coming year we are staying at an even bigger cabin, big enough for twenty-one people —seven families and a few singles.

Truthfully, Jerrie could still run to the top of Clingmans Dome, where we visited on our honeymoon, just a little slower. I'm slow so he walks with me. It's time to go again. Three of the great-grandchildren have not been to the top.

Now when we go to a cabin in Wears Valley, Tennessee (where we stay now instead of Gatlinburg), we stop and get pizza. By then we have eaten two good meals, and then we get to the cabin. Some go shopping for breakfast foods and snacks. The next morning, we get up and do as each person pleases. Each family goes their separate ways to shop or sightsee. We meet at a set time for dinner each night during the week, and then go our separate ways again.

When everyone gets in, we sometimes have a devotional period or singing and we talk about the next day (when and where to eat, etc.). As we leave to go home on Saturday morning, we decide who gets what of the leftover food. We stop at a favorite place for breakfast. A few hours later, we meet for lunch, hug and kiss each other bye, and everyone goes on home. These were days that were so worth the time and money. Wonderful, wonderful memories.

Annual family picnic in the Smokies

Chapter 27

Daddy's Death

"As a mother comforts her child, so will I comfort you."
—Isaiah 66:13

On Christmas Eve of 1976, we went to Daddy's house to stay for two days. It was one of those times when *everyone* was there, including all of Frances's children and all of Daddy's children and eleven grandchildren. Wayne, Frances, Frances's son, plus Frances's daughter and her three small boys were all still living at home with him.

We had a wonderful day together swapping stories. We reminisced about Mama, old times, funny times, life-changing poignant times, and times that taught us something.

That evening, I kissed Daddy on the cheek and saw him to bed. We all ate breakfast the next morning before Jerrie and I decided to take the children and pay a visit to Childhaven to spend a night or two. Our children always loved visiting.

The moment we arrived, Dot, the lady at the main office, told me I needed to call Daddy's house immediately. Evidently, we'd only been gone a few minutes when he'd gotten up to go to the bathroom and fell dead in the hallway. I was not very sad. I was surprised to find I was overcome with a sense of peace. I wondered who could have asked for a better day to die than on Christmas Day, surrounded by family.

A few days later, Daddy was buried in the churchyard next to Mama. I saw a lot of relatives I had not seen since I was a child. Some I remembered, though their faces had aged and grown less recognizable with time. They were deeply saddened by the loss of Daddy. Frances's children were devastated beyond belief. Like my siblings and I, they were affected by the early loss of a parent. Their biological father had been killed in a tragic automobile accident. Daddy, with all his charm and wit, had been their daddy, too.

When we were children at Childhaven, Brenda, Don, and I would sometimes visit Daddy and Frances. The two families never blended well, but we all had one thing in common: we loved Daddy. It never fully occurred to me that the children there were my *stepsiblings*—largely because I barely knew them. Brenda and Don and I had made Childhaven our home. As a child, I had wished we could be back with Daddy and Wayne, or more often, they could be with us.

But on that day, as we sat there in all black, commemorating Daddy, I looked up at the big, white, fleecy clouds, thinking about all the years of loss. I realized that despite the grief, I contentedly believed *everything is exactly as it should be.*

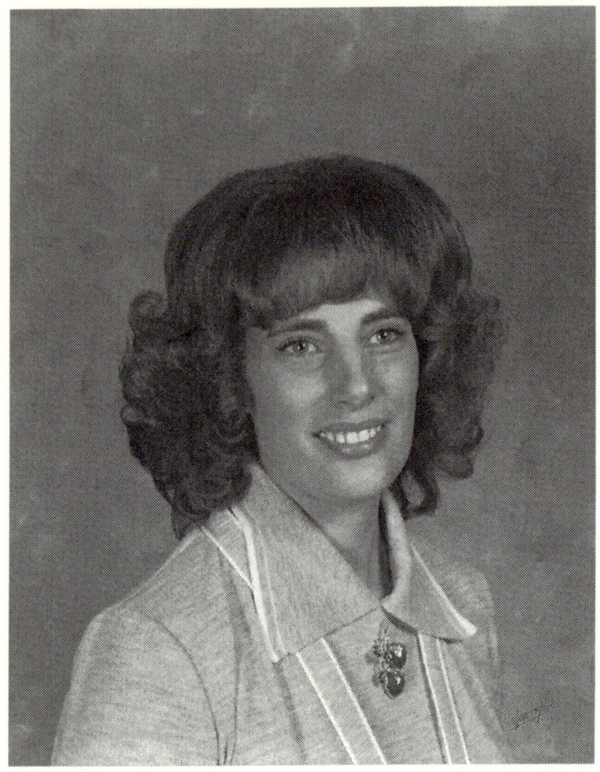

1976, Gail at thirty-three years of age

Chapter 28

The Blessings of Being in Ministry

"How wonderful it is that nobody need wait a single moment before starting to improve the world."
—Anne Frank

Since I came to Childhaven, I have loved to go to church and listen to preachers. Some of the greatest preachers held gospel meetings at our congregation in town. We had a guest room where they stayed. Daddy Brock was an excellent preacher. His favorite sermon was "Come Over Here and Help Us," from Acts 16:6–15, sometimes called the "Macedonian Call." Then he would ask the church to help Childhaven.

When we were college students, many of the "preacher boys" would go on Sundays to smaller congregations that couldn't afford a full-time preacher. Jerrie preached at four of the small churches in the area in the three years we were in school together.

Freed-Hardeman, a junior college at the time, had a third-year program for Bible majors. Jerrie went for three years to Freed-Hardeman and then three-quarters to Lipscomb University in Nashville, Tennessee, to finish his bachelor's degree. Once he graduated, one of those churches, Yorkville Church of Christ in Yorkville, Tennessee, invited him to be their preacher. They never had a full-time preacher living in the community.

When Jerrie had been there for about a year, he asked the elders if he could take off a week during the Christmas holidays. They agreed. He had very few agreements and didn't have a contract. I was concerned about how we were going to make the car payment.

The Sunday before, an elder stood before the church and said several people had given money for

Jerrie's Christmas present. He was given an envelope with thirty dollars in it.

I asked Jerrie, "What are you going to do with your Christmas money?" He said he would like to buy a pair of Sunday shoes because his were old, had holes in them, and weren't worth fixing.

I told Jerrie the church would not pay him for the Sunday he was gone. I was right. That's where Jerrie began learning about contracts and how to be clear on expectations. Jerrie always said, "We shared a lot of ignorance."

We made good friends there. Most nights we would go to someone's house to visit, eat popcorn, and drink Double Colas. Two members of the church sold the cola to grocery stores. They would give members a special discount, only charging them what they had paid for them, one dollar and twenty-five cents for a twenty-four-bottle case.

Jerrie Wayne was born while we lived in Yorkville, Tennessee. But there were brown recluse spiders everywhere. We were terrified that Jerrie Wayne would be bitten by one. A lot of mornings there would be half a dozen or more in our bathtub. I would clamp a fruit jar over one and it would jump up in the jar. I would put a lid on the jar and take it to the local school so the children could see what they needed to avoid.

While there, I had helped with community activities. The mayor of the town had asked my assistance on two occasions involving families with children.

I was named "Woman of the Year" and given a very beautiful cameo necklace. I felt extremely honored.

One of Gail's paintings. She and Jerrie printed them and sent them for birthday and anniversary cards.

When Jerrie Wayne was three months old, we were invited to a much larger congregation in Madisonville, Kentucky. We had a lovely house in a new subdivision. Christi was born while we were there. We worked with that church eight and a half years. The children were very happy. Our work was wonderful. Friends were abundant. Jerrie worked hard for the church. I got involved in community and school activities.

Then we heard that a church in Dalton, Georgia, had been without a preacher for several months. An elder and his wife called and wanted to come visit us. After driving to Dalton and much discussion, they invited us to come work with the church. We did. Dalton is where our children grew up, and the place they call home when asked where they are from.

We built a house in the country, raised our children, and helped many others with theirs. We had cows. We liked raising our own meat. We would have two slaughtered at a time—one the usual way for steaks and roast, and the other all hamburger. We had two large freezers for meat and vegetables. We often had four or five families over for Sunday dinner. We always had hamburgers. I also froze and canned food, including vegetables, jellies, and jam.

The Krystal hamburger restaurant was across the street from the church building. One Sunday, I guess as a joke, someone called in an order for a hundred burgers but never came to get them. When they saw our services were over, they called the church and asked to speak to me. Did I want the burgers? They knew what I did. They gave them to us for free.

We worked at that church eleven years.

Chapter 29

Emergency Medical Training

"It's been said that peace is not the absence of danger but the presence of God."
—Anne Graham Lotz

In 1964, our first married year at Freed-Hardeman, I decided to take a night course in emergency medical assistance. Then, it was called MEL, but now it's known as EMT. It served me well at accidents on the highway and emergencies in other places, but mostly with our own family.

We had lived in a city during our children's early years. They were six and nine when we built the house in the country. We had a large attic fan that could sometimes get loud. One night when Jerrie was out of town, the fan woke me up. I got up to turn it off. The noise didn't stop. The switch was just outside Jerrie Wayne's room. I realized he was making the noise. I did a check and knew we had to get to the hospital as quickly as possible.

I called the ER to let them know his condition and that we would be there in less than ten minutes. The doctor was waiting for us and took him from my arms. He was rushed into a room. I followed with Christi close behind. Jerrie Wayne's blood pressure was very low. His breathing was labored. They started him on oxygen and did an X-ray to see how much fluid was in his lungs. His lungs didn't look bad. We stayed the rest of the night and went home in the morning with medication.

That same day, I was cooking supper. Jerrie Wayne and Christi were watching TV cartoons. Jerrie Wayne got tickled about something and stopped breathing. There was no 911. I shook him and hit his chest with my fist. He took a little breath.

I told the phone operator to call the hospital and then connect to the ER and tell them a child is dying. A doctor came on. Christi was holding the phone to my ear as I was tending to Jerrie Wayne. I had gotten him breathing enough to stay alive.

When we got to the hospital, they went through the same routine as before. Blood pressure was low. Breathing labored. They gave him a treatment that opened his breathing passages. After several hours, he was fine. They told us he was allergic to the country atmosphere. Neighbors had cut hay the day before.

Soon after that episode, an old person suggested we give him local honey. We read about it and started him on two tablespoons a day. That fall, we made seven trips to either the ER or to his doctor. I had some emergency supplies the doctor gave me. Honey was our number one "medicine."

Jerrie Wayne did well until the next fall but did much better than the first year. Every year, he did better. He ate honey until he was grown. Jerrie, who often had sinus problems, started eating it also. Jerrie still does, every day, and never has any sinus problems.

Jerrie Wayne sported those striking blue eyes until he got the breath knocked out of him with a case of mononucleosis at eight years old. After weeks of being very ill, I noticed his eyes had dulled in color.

Though Jerrie Wayne was still beautiful, I missed the sparkly expressions that had been in his eyes when he was younger.

I was able to make a difference in at least a dozen bad accidents. Passersby want to help but are mostly harmful if they aren't trained.

In Crow Valley where we lived in Dalton, Georgia, there were three places I could see from the house that were very dangerous when it rained. One very stormy day, Jerrie Wayne and his best bud Norman were outside playing when they heard an accident nearby and ran to it. They ran back to the house and told me, "It's bad. Someone's going to kill them if you don't come." I gathered up some of the emergency equipment I kept at home, like insulated blankets and mouth-to-mouth pieces.

They were right. It was bad—a head-on collision between a jeep and a van. The lady in the van wasn't hurt much. She had picked up dozens of salads from a restaurant in carryout boxes for a family occasion. I think they all popped open because salad was everywhere, even on her. The smell of Thousand Island dressing made me feel sick.

The two men in the jeep, an elderly father and middle-aged son, were badly hurt. The son had been thrown out and was lying in the grass near a ditch. The jeep had turned on its side. Gas was running freely into the water-filled ditch. I told the boys to make sure no one smoked near the vehicles as more passersby stopped to help.

I knew some of the son's ribs were broken. From instinct, I guess, he was holding his left arm up with his right. I had someone hold it for him. He told me he was going to throw up and I said, "You are not! Breathe as deep as possible through your nose." It did the trick.

The man holding the younger man's arm softly said, "Gail, I am about to pass out."

I said, "Don't you dare pass out!" If he dropped the man's arm, his broken rib could go into his lung. When I found someone to take his place, the man went and laid down in the back seat of his car.

Everyone asked what they could do. I continued to say, "Don't let anyone smoke!" I went to check on the dad. I was sure the dad's back and maybe his neck were broken. He could move his fingers and toes a little, but not his head. He was worried about his son.

Someone called for an ambulance. Since we had only one emergency medical service in the area, it didn't surprise me that the first responders had to work another call first. But they did deliver a backboard and some blankets, and promised to return as soon as possible. All I could do while waiting for them was to try to keep the injured men warm. I didn't dare move either of them. Finally, a doctor on his way home stopped and stayed. He agreed not to move the father or the son, even with the backboard. After what seemed like hours, the medics came back.

By now, a crowd had gathered. We were all soaking wet and cold. The paramedics got the two men into two ambulances. They took the son to our local hospital and the dad to Erlanger, in Chattanooga, Tennessee, about thirty miles away. Then the paramedics asked if *I would tell the family*. They just didn't have time. So, I did.

The next day I went to see the son. He cried and thanked me and said he had never been so scared. But he hadn't heard from his dad. I didn't tell him what I was thinking: that his father, who was eighty or so years old, might have died.

About six months later, I was at the grocery store when I noticed an old man and woman talking and pointing at me. They started coming my way, so I went to meet them. It was the dad. He had broken his back, but he was up and buying groceries. I was so happy for him! The son had completely recovered.

I was coming home from work when an ambulance turned onto the road in front of me. I knew of a sick church member on the next road, but they passed it. I followed to a neighbor's house. I went in behind them. He, a most excellent neighbor and friend, had just killed himself. He had been told by his doctor he had cancer. He had seen his brother slowly die from cancer, and he made an announcement, "I will never die that way." He wasn't even sick with it yet and could have lived a long time. But when he heard the word cancer, he went crazy. Not thinking of family and friends, he walked in the house, took out a gun, and shot himself in the head, right in front of his wife.

I was able to help his wife and then his sons cope as they came home. The main question they had for me was can a person who commits suicide go to heaven. I told them I thought God was in charge of that and reminded them of Samson and King Saul.

On two occasions at Walmart, ladies passed out. The managers called for me, knowing I was in the store. One woman collapsed when I was within a few feet of her.

It felt good to have enough knowledge to be helpful and enough willingness and love to provide comfort.

Mark, a teen in our church and a dear neighbor, was in a terrible automobile accident. His beautiful face was cut all over in slashes, some crisscrossing. One bad cut had several other cuts that crossed it.

Two weeks later, Jerrie, Jerrie Wayne and I were in Jamaica doing mission work. When we got home, Mark called me and told me he hadn't wanted the doctor to take the stitches out. He told the doctor, "I will wait for Ms. Gail, the preacher's wife, to take them out."

I had a stitch removal kit a doctor had given me for some reason. Every day for weeks after school, he would come by our house. I would remove twenty or so stitches of the two hundred-plus that were in his face. The crisscrosses were very difficult and had a higher risk of scarring.

When I finally got all the stiches out, his beautiful face was restored. The doctor had done an excellent job stitching. I was pleased with the result.

Chapter 30

Raising Preacher's Children

"Don't criticize yourself for not being perfect. Give yourself time to grow knowing that you are enough . . . just the way you are."
—Anonymous

Like their births and bill of health growing up, our children's personalities were very different. Christi was made of caution, and Jerrie Wayne was built for adventure. If there was a puddle of water, Christi would go around it, but Jerrie Wayne would walk through it.

Our driveway had been laid out in sections. Jerrie and I had one rule: *do not* cross the line at the end of the driveway into the street. Naturally, Jerrie Wayne would do anything to rush to the edge of the driveway and put one foot over the line, while Christi would step back from it. In between hospital visits, she had no desire to be disciplined. She wanted to behave.

Their early years as preacher's children were easy, though they lived under the microscope of the community. If they misbehaved, we were immediately told. If they did something sweet and endearing, we were told that, too.

Their teen years were certainly more difficult, especially for Jerrie Wayne. He lived his life as a natural enthusiast and a trendsetter. If he shaved his head, others did, too. He loved wearing loud, offbeat clothing, like pants with lots of pockets paired with vibrantly colored shirts.

Although we had taken a trip to Israel during that time, there was one mission trip to Jamaica that was memorable, especially in our son's life. It was his first time out of the country and in a different culture.

We had one day to go to the market. Jerrie Wayne was a tall, skinny, white-haired boy. We didn't feel any threat and he didn't either, so we just let him walk around on his own. When it was time to go back to the hotel, he came out of the market and wasn't wearing one garment he'd gone in wearing. He had gone in with one kind of cap, had come out with a hat, and just had the best time. He had traded all his clothes for some of their clothes. He absolutely loved his new clothes. He's a trader. All his life he has been a trader.

Once, a man approached Jerrie at church and said, "I don't like the way Jerrie Wayne dresses."

Jerrie said, "Neither do I."

Then the man asked, "What are you going to do about it?"

"Nothing," Jerrie responded. "We may have lots of battles ahead. This one isn't worth fighting." That's what always made Jerrie such a great parent.

One of our main family rules was: *Do nothing to bring shame on the church or our family name.* The children would abide by that most of the time.

Once, when Christi was in high school, she and some friends decided to share one cigarette. She told her best friend Allison, who took it upon herself to tell other students Christi was smoking. Finally, Christi told her, "You meet me at my house after school, and we are going to fight this out because we can't do it at school and bring shame to our name or the church." Allison lived across the street and went to church with us.

Christi called me from school and said, "Mama, don't be surprised at what happens when I get home. Just go along with me."

I had no idea what she was talking about until she got off the bus followed by six cars and trucks full of students coming to see the fight. Allison came stomping from her house and Christi walked angrily toward her. When they finally met each other, they stood still facing each other for a minute, then hugged each other and started apologizing to each other.

The students were yelling, "No! Come on! Fight!"

But that just wasn't their way. They had already made up at school and planned this whole thing.

In retrospect, it's comedic. Our daughter's character has always preceded her, and that makes me proud.

When we moved to Nashville, Tennessee, Jerrie Wayne was in college at Freed-Hardeman. Christi was a senior in high school. We had put her in a Christian school because it was smaller than public school. We thought she could make friends quicker there, which she did. Again, our house quickly became the gathering place in our new hometown.

One day, I had just taken a large pan of cornbread out of the oven. One of the boys asked, "Mrs. Gail, is that a cake?"

I said, "No, it's cornbread. Do you want some?"

He said, "Yes."

The group ate the whole thing. It became their favorite thing for me to fix for them.

Christi had a great year and then went on to Freed-Hardeman. She was a "pretty young thing." Soon after her arrival, too many boys approached her at the same time. She saw Jerrie Wayne in the distance and yelled, "Brother!" as she always did when she needed him. He came running and said, "Back off, boys. She's going to be here a while." It made me smile to realize they were as close as Don and Brenda and I had been while in school together.

Christi pursued her dream of becoming a schoolteacher and has the grace-filled, beautiful life we wanted for her. She married a local boy, a fellow church member. Today, they have two grown children, Brittan and Braden. Brittan is married.

I inherited Mama's love of sewing. Like Mama, I've always had a deep affinity for threadwork. Whether it was on a machine or sitting down with a quilt—it felt meditative for me.

In high school, I took a lot of Home Economics classes. In college, I learned to tailor and make my own patterns.

I made bridesmaid dresses for both our children's weddings.

After graduating, Jerrie Wayne married a preacher's daughter and moved near Albany, New York. We were devastated when his wife was unfaithful to the marriage, and they divorced. To heal his heart, Jerrie Wayne returned to our home in Nashville and got a job. He was introduced to a lovely woman with two children who had also been betrayed by her previous spouse. Soon after, they married.

He adopted her daughters Elizabeth and Whitney, aged three and eight. They love him like children love their dads. They also have two boys: Dalton and Wyatt Houston. All his children are married except Wyatt Houston. Jerrie Wayne has five grandchildren.

One of them, Connor, is amazing. He was born with a deformity in his back. His medical care and operations have been heavily supported by the church and fundraisers. Early in his life, he received surgery. Afterward, a video was taken of the first time he walked after his operations. All the way through the recording, he is crying in extreme pain and saying, "Oh! Oh! Oh!" occasionally crying, "Papa help me," as he walks away from his bed and then returns to it—all the while wearing a fourteen-pound halo on his head. He will spend the rest of his life celebrating his mobility, and we will celebrate with him.

Connor playing basketball

Often when Jerrie leads a leadership workshop, he will show them that video of Connor, and say, “Why would two good Christian parents allow their child to hurt like that? They didn’t have to do that. They could have put him in a recliner and let him play video games instead of walking.” Of course, the obvious reason is that that is what it takes to get him to where he can walk again. Jerrie then says, “That’s my purpose this weekend. I’m going to try to make you very uncomfortable so you will be better at the end.” And with that, there’s an instant understanding at the workshop that growth isn't always comfortable, but it is for our own good.

One of my favorite memories is of another boy named Connor and his mother. I had a signature perfume as a young person, one that I wore every single Sunday (and still wear to this day). I wanted the children to think of me when they smelled it, wherever they were or however old they were.

One day I was in Walmart when I heard a familiar child's voice yelling, "Mrs. Gail, Mrs. Gail, Mrs. Gail." I started looking for the voice and ran into Connor. He was out of breath, with his mother close behind. We were hugging each other when his mother asked him, "How did you know she was in here?"

"I could smell her," he answered.

Embarrassed, she said, "Oh, Connor."

When I explained it was my perfume he smelled, she was relieved.

Years after college, Jerrie Wayne was asked to be on the Freed-Hardeman advisory board. Jerrie and I have had the opportunity to speak at the university's annual lectureships. It's become a family tradition—four of our grandchildren have now gone to their parents' alma mater.

Today, Jerrie Wayne celebrates that his grandson is much better. Connor's back is held together with titanium rods and spikes. He is fine now and playing on a basketball team. He's already broken those rods two or three times because he is so active. He is an astoundingly resilient little thing—physically but also in spirit. Throughout every operation, he has made the best of it.

Connor and his parents understand the glory of God and have been raised in the brightest of spirits. They have always been grateful to Scottish Rite Hospital and Ronald McDonald House for their part.

Chapter 31

Interim Ministry

"Live, love, laugh, learn, leave."
—My motto for interim ministry

We had been at the West Nashville Church of Christ for five years, from 1988–1993, when two elders of the Berry's Chapel Church of Christ called Jerrie and asked him to have a meal with them.

"We need you. Would you come work with us?" We agreed to go to Franklin, Tennessee. One of the good things about the change was it was close enough for us to stay in the house we had built when we first came to Nashville. It was a wonderful work.

During our marriage, Jerrie and I served five churches on a full-time basis. After about eleven years of this work, Jerrie informed the elders that we were planning to start an interim ministry in about three years. Interim ministry work is not common in the Church of Christ. Jerrie and I went for training on the basics of it in Atlanta, Georgia, at the Simpsonwood Retreat Center.

In 2007, we started interim ministry. Keeping our house in Nashville, we began working with congregations in various cities, staying from six to eighteen months with each place.

When people ask us about what we do, Jerrie says, “When a preacher stays a long time with a church and then leaves, some people don’t like the next preacher. I volunteer to be that preacher, but they will like me because I’m not there to take anyone’s place, but to help them get ready for their next full-time preacher.” We love the impact we make at every stop and the impact they make on us.

Our first interim was in Eddyville, Kentucky, a church of about sixty-five people. They called it New Eddyville. The old town had been flooded to build a dam. The people could still point to where their house had been. We already had good friends there. Their young people had gone to camp with ours.

After fifteen months there, we worked with the Hendersonville Church, with a membership of about fifteen hundred. The first Sunday, a man approached me and asked if I was in shock.

I said, "No. Why do you ask?"

He said, "This is a huge crowd." I told him I had been in crowds before, and it didn't bother me.

We couldn't possibly get to know or even speak to everyone, but we did get involved with a group of older members who called themselves "Senior Moments."

After fourteen months there, we worked with the Collegeside Church of Christ in Cookeville, Tennessee. Tennessee Tech was two blocks over. The church did an excellent job with students there. They had a building on our church property where students could meet to study, have devotionals, play games, and eat.

Lavergne, Tennessee, was next. They were hurting because the preacher and about half of the congregation had left. We stayed with them two years. They have a good young man working with them now and doing great work for God.

Maury City Church of Christ in Friendship, Tennessee, had experienced much the same. Their membership was small. They had a nice house next to the church building with a yard large enough for me to grow a garden and have a lot of flowers. A man who has become our good friend came to work with them.

Northside Church of Christ in Jeffersonville, Indiana, was the farthest from home we had been. They also had a children's care organization and seven very nice houses for older members. Jerrie jokes, "They broke the rules and let us move in." I enjoyed being at that church very much.

Shady Acres Church of Christ in Sikeston, Missouri, was next. They had released their longtime preacher. Some were very unhappy about it. Some were happy. I made friends quickly, starting with the first Sunday when a man teasingly pointed to a seat and said, "That's my seat." I sat in front of him. I became fast friends with him and his wife.

After we'd been there a while, he asked me one Sunday, "How do we rank in the churches you have worked with?"

I quickly responded, "Second."

He said, "WE DO NOT!" They didn't. They were the best.

We were invited to work with the River Road Church of Christ, one and a half miles from our house in Nashville. Moving back home was our hardest move as we also had all the things we'd accumulated as we moved from place to place. I called my children and told them I was going to give them a great gift: a grand sweep of the house so they wouldn't have so much to do when we died. If it was a drawer or door, it was opened. There were three choices: give away, throw away, or keep. Some things were hard to let go. But it was done.

We then went to the Central Church of Christ in McMinnville, Tennessee, just as COVID-19 hit. I love to be at a church where there are lots of activities during the week. All these things had to be canceled. Staying at home was so hard and boring.

Before we left there, the church gave us a great dinner to celebrate Jerrie's sixty years of preaching. Our children gave wonderful talks on what it is like to be a P.K. (preacher's kid). People came from other churches where we had been. It was like having our funeral while we were still living, an excellent day of celebration.

As of this writing we are working with the Pacific Church of Christ in Pacific, Missouri. Their membership is small. I don't think we have worked with a harder-working group. They give liberally of their time, money, and love. We have been here one year and are looking forward to several more months. They have a nice house next to the church building, which is home to maybe a thousand moles and about half that many squirrels. I think my garden will be in pots this time.

We always look forward to every adventure. In between interims, we take two months to rest, recuperate, and go on vacation, usually a place a church member suggests. All have been enjoyable for us.

When we were young, we did a lot of outdoor things, like mountain climbing, white water rafting, and walking through parks. We do more driving now, just wondering at God's wonderful creation.

At the time of this writing in 2022, we have worked with ten interim congregations over the last fifteen years. We love it! We have met so many wonderful Christian people who are now our friends. Jerrie always says, "I never met an interim I didn't like."

As our family expands, our church family continues to grow. Our journey has helped us build relationships with more than five thousand people. God uses us in new ways. We are challenged and refined by our love for ministry and the outstanding people of our church who fuel our desire to *make a difference*.

We pray God allows us to live and be healthy enough to serve several more churches.

Chapter 32

Making a Difference

"The purpose of life is not to be happy.
It is to be useful, to be honorable, to be compassionate,
to have it make some difference that
you have lived and lived well."
—Ralph Waldo Emerson

Making a difference costs time, money, and resources. Part of our ministry is heeding that call when it comes. Jerrie and I have learned to navigate devastating situations that require God's help to recover from.

When our children were young, a teen in our congregation was hooked on drugs. The church elders unanimously agreed to send him to rehab. After being in rehab for a few weeks, he took Tylenol

#2 (Tylenol plus Codeine) and was forced to leave the program for one month, return, and start over. While he was home, no one wanted him to go to his own house or his friends' houses for fear he would be too tempted. During that time, Jerrie and I decided he could live with us.

We had a guest bedroom in the basement, complete with a bathroom. Some church members criticized us, some praised us. One man said with a judgmental tone, "I just don't understand how you could bring a boy *like him* into your house with your young children. Aren't you afraid at all?"

"No," I said. "We've had a long talk about rules. One of them being, 'If I catch you doing anything to harm our children, I will kill you.'" Another one of our rules was no radio or TV on during meals so we can talk to each other.

Surprisingly, the boy not only loved our rules, but enjoyed being a part of our family rituals. He loved talking as we ate. He was very funny, a quality no one ever knew about, not even him! In turn, our children quickly grew to love him. After one month of excellent conversation, warm laughter, and recovery, he returned to rehab and did very well.

We moved from that house but were determined to stay connected to him. We sent him a birthday card every year. Over time he moved to another state, got a good job, married, and had children. This important experience gave us the knowledge we would need for the ensuing years in our ministry. We all felt we had made a difference.

A few years later, Ben, another teen in our church, started doing drugs. He was popular and had money and influence. He and our children were members of our large, active youth group.

I asked Ben if we could talk. I knew the signs of drug use, and I knew how to be direct. I told him I knew what he was doing. I told him he was no longer to ride with our children to any youth event, nor could our children ride in his car. He was never to be alone with our children under any circumstances. I gave the children the same rule. He agreed and said he understood.

A few weeks after, his parents called and asked us to be at their house the next morning at 6 a.m.

They said people from rehab were going to be there to intervene. They woke him from his sleep and took him out, kicking and screaming. Though his exit was turbulent, his rehab progress appeared to be excellent.

When he returned home, he asked for forgiveness and prayers from the church to stay clean. Our children wanted to know if the same rules still applied about car rides.

"Absolutely," we insisted. They were confused by this, wondering why the rule stood if we truly forgave Ben. Jerrie and I explained that forgiveness doesn't overrule discernment and boundaries.

Three months passed, and I believed Ben was on the right path. So, I decided to do something. At our church, we always kept bookmarks in the songbook holder. I'd often write little notes to people on the backs of them. Using one of them, I wrote to Ben, "You are now the kind of person I would be proud for my children to call a friend." I casually handed it to him in passing.

A few days, later, his mother called and asked if I would come to their house. I initially feared the worst. When I arrived, she took me to Ben's room. On the wall was my note, framed in a 14-by-20 frame. It was matted with that little handwritten note in the center. Ben had asked her to do it.

I like to believe my little note and big faith were part of what made a difference for him. He certainly made an impact on me.

Joe, Bobby, and their baby stepbrother Jimmy had gone to church with us for about a year. They all sat in the row in front of us at church. Since their parents had been killed in the same accident, they had lived with Joe and Bobby's step-grandparents.

It was easy to see that Joe and Bobby's step-grandparents gave most of their love to Jimmy. Jimmy was their only blood relative, their only son's child. The two older boys were their daughter-in-law's children from a previous marriage. Joe and Bobby were soon sent to military school.

Joe excelled. He was a natural leader. Bobby didn't do as well. After a year in military school, their grandparents decided that it would be good for them to go to Childhaven, because of me and the way I had turned out. Joe also became a leader there, nicknamed "Sergeant."

When Joe was sixteen, he asked his "grandparents" if he could come home to finish high school. They said no. But they did ask our congregation if there was anyone who would take him. That Sunday, Jerrie preached "God requires action and not excuses." We decided to let Joe live with us, but only through child protective services, so we could officially be his foster parents. That way they would give us a little money for clothes and food.

When he moved in, Christi was three weeks old, and we had just celebrated Jerrie Wayne's third birthday. Jerrie Wayne adored him. Christi, in time, came to love him.

Joe was a kindred spirit to me. I knew we wouldn't have any major problems. He fit very well into the youth group and school. He quickly became the boy other boys wanted to be with—a man's man, though he wasn't very big.

I was only eight years older than Joe. We even resembled each other slightly. When we were out to eat or shopping, he would call me “Mama” just to see the expression on people’s faces.

When he graduated from high school, he decided to go into the army. Jerrie took him to the recruiting office. He was still seven months away from being eighteen, but they allowed him to join. When they asked him his full name, he didn’t know it, but we were able to get that information from a relative who lived in town. He served the army well as a sergeant for twenty years.

He married. They had one girl. He served as a deacon in a church. He also spent five years in the U.S. Secret Service. He was then an ROTC instructor at a high school.

Joe had to go to serve in Operation Desert Storm. Not knowing the outcome, he sent us a cassette tape thanking us and telling us we had made a big difference in his life.

After he returned safely, we spoke to him several times by phone. He was proud of himself. Bobby had done well for himself.

Joe called one day in 2016 to tell us he had been diagnosed with an aggressive cancer and had no chance of surviving it. He told us that his house was paid for and that his daughter would graduate from college with no debt. His wife would have no financial worries. He felt good leaving all well.

We had several foster children after Joe, but none as long. Once we had two brothers and a sister. I enjoyed foster care, but we gave it up when we moved to Georgia.

Joe Hatchel who lived with us for a year and a half as a foster child

Once I was teaching a class of about forty ladies. The subject was "loving yourself and other people the way God loves us." The teacher's manual included a list of questions that were to be filled out by each person and then turned back in to me.

One of the questions was, *Have you ever abused anyone?*

The next question was, *Has anyone ever abused you?*

All the papers but one answered *no* and *no* to the two questions. But one woman wrote, "Every day my husband abuses me physically or verbally, and sometimes both."

To address the issue, I said to the class, "One of you is hurting because of physical and mental abuse. If you want to let me know in some way, I will do anything I can to help you if you want me to." I was hoping the woman would come to speak with me.

When the class was over, the ladies were telling me how much they enjoyed the class. Some hugged me. Then, in a quiet moment, one woman grabbed my hand tightly, looked me in the eye, and nodded her head to say, *yes*. I hugged her and held back the tears for her sake.

I was especially surprised at this news because the woman and her husband seemed very close. He typically sat with his arm around her in the pew. They were always together at functions.

I began hugging the woman very intentionally. I am a talker and a hugger, so her husband didn't seem to make anything out of me hugging her. During the hug, I would whisper, "How was your week?" and she would respond by giving me a number from one to ten that described how bad it was: nine, seven, five. In response, I'd always hold her hand a little longer.

After our lessons, her husband always came to the classroom area to get her. Once, when he wasn't there yet, I asked her if she ever considered fighting back—perhaps with a weapon, to emphasize, *You are not going to hurt me today*. She said she was too frightened to do it. So, we took to praying instead.

Ironically (and horrifyingly), he was later killed in an automobile accident. She about cried her heart out at the funeral. Though she may have loved him at one time, I knew they were tears of joy and release.

The next Sunday, she walked with more liberation than I'd ever seen. She sat in a different pew—smiling, talking freely with people, and accepting the words of sympathy without ever mentioning her abuse. People thought they were really in love. I knew enough from Mammy to know that *true love doesn't hurt.* I try really, really hard to drive that message home with all of the women I teach.

My upbringing instilled in me the idea that because God loves us, we must also love ourselves. Several of the biggest spiritual struggles in our church were individuals at war with themselves. As the poster says, "God made me and God don't make no junk."

On one occasion, I got a call that one of the women in our church was threatening suicide. Evidently, she put a knife to her neck and said she would use it if *I* didn't come to help her.

This made me sad and frightened. So, I agreed to come if I could bring Stan, a police friend, with me. The woman insisted, "Please, no police." I finally got her to agree. After I got there, I found her sitting on her bed weeping with a butcher knife against her jugular vein.

Her family members surrounded her, trying to comfort her. After a moment or so, I walked into the room and held out my hand for the knife. She dropped it on the floor and collapsed in my arms, totally exhausted. I had already instructed someone to call for an ambulance. Once at the local hospital, she was admitted to the mental ward for recovery.

When Christi and Jerrie Wayne were still living at home, we had a neighbor who had a toddler around two years old who seemed to have learning problems—possibly physical ones too. He was a very stiff child who was hard to hold and who didn't speak. Though we weren't close friends, his mother, in a bind one day, asked me if I could watch him.

My children started to play with him. Pretty soon, he was running all over laughing and happily playing. We certainly had fun together when he was in my care. We visited friends who had an aquarium, fish, and a bubble-making machine in the water. I would say, "fish . . . bubbles!" It wasn't long until he was repeating both words. There were a few other words he picked up. He called Christi "Key Key." He was such a delight.

When I took him home that afternoon, he was very relaxed in my arms with his head on my shoulder and his arms around my neck. His mother commented, "I've never seen him so relaxed. He feels like *your* baby."

I nodded, as I tried to treat *every* child as if they were my own.

When I put him down, he ran to their aquarium and said, "Fish . . . bubbles," over and over.

His Mom was so amazed, she sat down and started to cry. "What have I done wrong to this child? What have you done right?"

I knew I had to be careful with my answer—it was such a good teaching moment. "God, help me," I prayed silently as I waited for her to calm down and stop crying.

Finally, when he came to me instead of her, I knew.

"I believe you are a terrified mother," I told her. "You are afraid of doing the wrong thing. You are so uptight about him, and you make him the same way. He *feels* you. I am loose and relaxed. He feels that. You have got to find a way to relax, even if it means you need to get professional help." Thankfully, the mother received my words well. I was pleased to learn later that they were deeply helpful to her.

50th Wedding Anniversary, August 18, 2014

As of this writing, I am seventy-nine years old. I've taught many Bible classes, especially to little children. Perhaps it's my ego, but I want them to look back when they are old and remember that Mrs. Gail taught them that they were loved. Therefore, they should love God and others as well.

In the way I remember all the adults who raised me, I hope they remember me. I hope I can give them the most substantial thing I have—the Word of God—to build a life upon. Because you will never, ever know who is watching you from afar. And you'll never know how many lives you'll touch simply by being yourself and doing your best.

Recently, Jerrie and I were in a restaurant. A man and woman came to our table and asked if we were *the Barbers*. I'm used to people knowing Jerrie. He's never met a stranger. He extended his hand, confirming that we were. The wife delightedly said, "I remember Mrs. Gail teaching my class at church camp."

Evidently, that camp had been her first summer away from her family. She'd been homesick and very unhappy. Then she came to me, and I picked her up and held her until she fell asleep. I helped her adjust, and she ended up finishing the week at camp. I had no memory of the event, but she did. When we went to pay for our tab, it had been paid. I figured something I'd contributed must have been worth it to her.

As we drove home, I thought about how blessed I am. I have a loving, supportive husband, two children who are wonderful, and six amazing grandchildren—four of whom are married, and five great-grandchildren. I pray they all live their lives to please God, the way Mother Lee and Daddy Brock prayed for me when I was young, blessing the wonderful life I have today.

These beautiful and refining experiences grew our capacity in the ministry to show up for others, even when we didn't yet understand what they needed.

But the most impactful part of showing up for others often happened when *I did* understand. The traumatic events that led me to James Jones are like many of the family issues we see in our church. I know when standing in a group of fifty people, my story will be relatable to *at least one,* if not several more.

When I was younger and darkness covered everything I knew to be true, I imagined myself beside Mama, reliving that day on the other side of the lake. In my mind, I'd curl up beneath the tree where she once napped and remember the last time I felt truly *full*—of baloney, of potato chips, of rest, of love.

When I worked with James Jones, I designated that tree as my safe space. It'd always been the easiest place to return to. I loved the fresh breeze and the warm sun. It was where I told Mama to go in her imagination when she was too sick to get out of bed. I would lie beside her for hours, rubbing her fragile arm, as sick in my spirit as she was in her body.

"Mama, don't think about the hurt—think about the other side of the lake. You'll feel good there and you'll forget the pain." I like to pretend she listened.

One of Gail's paintings

Chapter 33

Was I Worth It?

"No matter what has happened to you in the past or what is going on in your life right now, it has no power to keep you from having an amazingly good future if you will walk by faith in God."
—Joyce Meyer

"When I was just a child of four and five, it was worth the price of giving up play to help Mama, just to hear Daddy say I was the best little girl in the whole wide world. My greatest desire was to please them and make them proud of me. I'm not sure I could have put it into words then, but I knew the feeling. I did what it took to never disappoint them. Even living with Mammy. I didn't want this compliment to go to waste." As I retold my story in intimate detail to James

Jones, he focused more on listening than writing anything down.

He twisted the toothpick he held between his clenched teeth—something that struck me as both annoying and endearing. Then he remarked about how he was impressed by my ability to cope as a child. How, when I was as young as five years old, I was raising my siblings out of the clutches of poverty, horrendous abuse, perpetual abandonment, and enduring grief.

He believed it was the love for my parents and siblings that fostered my survival instinct. He believed I had a will to live that was otherworldly.

When I remarked, "If it hadn't been for God . . ."

He agreed, but added, "*and Gail.* If it hadn't been for brazen, Little Gail, you would have never made it through."

My Aunt Dovie (who was really my cousin) always wrote me at least once or twice a year while I was at Childhaven. Years after I was married, I wrote my

Aunt Dovie and described the way I remembered living at Mammy's, thinking a child's memory might be exaggerated.

Her return letter said it was *a lot worse* than I remembered. I read her letter out loud in the car as Jerrie drove. My children were in the backseat. Aunt Dovie had listed everyone who had recently died. She wrote, "I lost Mama six years ago . . . I lost Kay two years ago . . . Last year I lost Betty . . ." and on and on. I was very familiar with loss but the way in which she listed all her sorrows one by one was a little over the top.

When I got through the letter, Christi, who was then six-years-old, said, "Mama, I know you don't know much about your family, but I can tell you this one is absent-minded." We had never used the term *lost for dead*. Children are often perceptive and funny!

Mammy died when I was twelve years old, although I didn't find out until sometime later. The last time we saw her was the day the welfare man took us away. I don't know how long Daddy and Wayne continued to live with her, but I assume they did for a while because it was free. She could help with Wayne while Daddy was at work. She was usually kind to Wayne, and I would assume even more so after we were gone and didn't aggravate her.

In the early 1990s, when our children were grown, I visited Mammy's house with Jerrie, Brenda, Don, and Wayne. When Mammy died, somebody acquired her house. They got all the wood that was in her house and built a little store in town. I wouldn't go inside. Those wooden planks had seen things no child should have to endure.

I was so glad that our children would never know the pain of growing up in an abusive household.

Champions at Childhaven

It had been over twenty years since I'd had a visit from Little Me, but I still thought about those visits from time to time. I initially believed it would be too *out there* to confide in James about Little Me, so I kept her to myself. By then I was comfortable talking about various aspects of my story, but I was concerned that he might think I was crazy or not believe me. I would tell him when the time was right.

Then on July 2, 1995, Jerrie and I received the tragic news: James had died in the night. He was found by his wife, sitting straight up in bed, with his signature wooden toothpick nestled in the corner of his mouth.

We were all devastated. Jerrie was heartbroken. Jerrie did James's funeral. He and James were great friends, probably best friends. They did workshops together and talked with each other often.

I grieved deeply. I had done my homework and had become more confident and comfortable in my own skin and around others. I had hoped we would continue this work for as long as we both felt I was benefiting from it. But it was not to be. I still wished we had talked about Little Me.

What would happen now? Would I be able to continue the work without his guidance? Or would I fall back to my old mindset and allow my fears to consume me?

I quickly decided that I would do everything I could to continue my work, overcome my debilitating anxiety, and lessen the frequency of—and perhaps stop altogether—my frightful dreams. I owed it to both myself and to James to keep moving forward. I had made a promise to Little Me and I was determined to keep it. We would *both* be all right.

Sometime after, James came to visit me one last time in a dream. He appeared just as I remembered him—with a bright smile and a glistening, bald head. Suddenly, Mammy appeared out of nowhere with an ax, attempting to whack him with it. With urgency, he looked at me and said, "Gail, she doesn't want me to make you well, but I'm going to." Then I woke, knowing even in death, he was still helping me.

James Jones was the one who gave me the strength to grieve the trauma of Mammy so when a teenager escaping their pain needs a place to recover, or when an abused woman needs to be held, or when a person is suffering so deeply they want to take their life, I have the appropriate skill set to love and support them. I believe this is how God made beauty out of ashes. He helped me learn from the brokenness of others and use my lessons as a catalyst to heal.

James Jones (L) and Jerrie (R)

The last time I saw Little Me was in the summer of 1988. She came to me smiling and lighthearted. I was so happy for her. I picked her up and held her over my head. She was light, both in weight and spirit. Afterward, we sat for a long time talking. I told her about the man I'd married and about our wonderful children. I told her about faith, and God, and the church.

"You will walk with kings," I promised her. "People who are important. People who love you. You are royalty."

We hugged and cuddled for a while. I kissed her soft cheek. She laid her head on my shoulder while we said nothing. The moment was bittersweet. I sensed it was a goodbye visit.

"Am I going to be all right?" she asked me, her head still on my shoulder.

"Yes," I assured her. It was a promise I could finally keep. While I had endured unbelievable trauma as a child, I was determined to live the best life I could and have a healthy, happy family.

Chapter 34

The Legacy of Childhaven

"Sing to the LORD a new song; sing to the LORD,
all the earth.
Sing to the LORD, bless his name;
proclaim his salvation day after day.
Tell his glory among the nations;
among all peoples, his marvelous deeds."
—Psalm 96:1-3

Childhaven has changed drastically since my childhood. When I was there, it was one big happy family in one big house. They didn't work with families to try to get the children back into the home like they do now. It was common for children to come at three or four years old and stay until they married, got a job, or went to college. Brenda, Don, and I grew up there. Then somebody paid for our education, and we went to college.

Even now, it is unbelievable to me that we were supported financially. It was as though the years of deficit in our early childhood were compensated for in our teens and early adulthood. Not only were we blessed, but our cup overflowed so we could delight in taking care of others the way the houseparents of Childhaven had taught us.

Today, Childhaven's services are specific to pregnant teens, or teenage mothers and their babies. The staff helps them learn life skills, such as how to balance a checkbook, and how to interview for a job. Some of them learn how to drive. Even though it is different, it is still fulfilling its purpose as a home for worthy children. They live in different houses on the property. The big house is mainly for administration.

Childhaven was the cornerstone that preserved my life as an adolescent. Though I believe I would have found my *true north* regardless, it would have not been without direct impact to my self-esteem. Mother Lee and Daddy Brock were continual pillars of support even after I was ushered into adulthood, and after marrying Jerrie. Even after the tragedy of Daddy Brock's being removed as superintendent, due to the boards' "progressive" opinion on what is considered manual labor.

After they left Childhaven, Mother Lee and Daddy Brock started a drive-through for fresh dairy and animal products, especially eggs that had come from their own chicken houses. They relied on the very thing they had taught all of us—how to make a living off the land. It was their intention to never see us struggle or claim welfare.

Before they left, Mother Lee and Daddy Brock bragged on me, so I carried out their best wishes for me, ensuring neither their compliments nor their efforts to see me thrive were wasted. I wanted people from my home church to see how my siblings and I turned out and believe that their time and investment in us had been worth it.

Many years after I'd been married to Jerrie and had children of our own, a lady who had moved from Florida came to our congregation in Dalton. When she learned I had been reared at Childhaven, she told me that all her life she'd sent five dollars a month to help support the children there. The longer we discussed my upbringing—the Christmases, the lavish gifts, and the yummy meals we'd been given—the more delighted she became, knowing that her small monthly donations had greatly contributed to my becoming the woman I am today.

It wasn't without a cost—the youth group at the 4th Street Church of Christ in Tuscumbia, Alabama, sent Brenda and me spare change for more than thirteen years. I can only imagine a fraction of a teenager's hard-earned allowance going to charity, without the young girls and boys ever knowing it mattered. *Every cent mattered.*

It taught me the value of money—that it should neither be squandered nor held too closely. Mother Lee and Daddy Brock taught us how to hold ourselves with dignity. We might have been *orphans,* but we never felt like it. We knew better than to act pitiful for money or for handouts or attention. After all, the way we acted directly represented our family. Besides the joy of making our houseparents proud, there was always the satisfaction of knowing my behavior would be bragged about to Daddy when he paid us a visit.

One of Gail's paintings

Daddy Brock passed away in the spring of 1989. (Mother Lee would go on to outlive him by twenty-one years.) One of the last conversations I had with their son, Del, meant the world to me. He asked me if I knew how much I was loved by both of his parents, but especially Daddy Brock.

"You know you were one of Dad's favorites," Del began. "Maybe his favorite of all." Del and the older boys called him "Coach" because he was. A former Howard College football star, Daddy Brock resigned in 1950 from his coaching position at the Southern Industrial Institute in Camp Hill, Alabama, to take over as the superintendent of Childhaven, a position he held for fourteen wonderful years.

I cried at the news of this, grieving the death of Daddy Brock. I was honored to know that he thought so fondly of me, even after so many years had passed.

Jerrie spoke at Daddy Brock's funeral. Many of "his" children were there. As I sat there, handkerchief in hand, grieving my second father, I evaluated everything about my life, hoping I had made him proud. It made me think about what it means to be a *good father*—and about the mercies of God the Father that I had seen since first arriving at Childhaven.

As early as my first Sunday at my new home at Childhaven, I began to learn about Jesus. Sometimes the stories of the gospel scared me. It was more than the crucifixion of Christ—it was the intense, radical, sacrificial love I saw in Jesus and His disciples. Like in the parables of Jesus, my childlike mind understood the gravity all too well of things I couldn't fully explain.

My first Bible class was taught by Mrs. Mildred Thompson—it was on the lesson of Judas betraying Jesus. I was scared by the imagery of it—especially the part where Judas took his own life, hanging himself until he was *broken asunder*. I had never heard that term before, but Mrs. Mildred explained what that meant—to be cracked apart by our own sin and darkness. It sounded awful, and gave me more than I could measure to think about.

After the lesson we went to worship. We all sat together. I was given a nickel by Mother Lee to put in a basket that was being passed down every aisle of the church. I was not yet allowed to eat the bread or drink the juice. At the end of service, everyone stood to sing "Blessed Be the Tie that Binds." "When we asunder part," the song says, "it gives us inward pain."

Yes, that would hurt. I thought.

Being a Christian in those days meant beyond obeying the commandments—we could neither dance nor swim in mixed company. We couldn't miss church under any circumstances. And certain substances, including cigarettes and alcohol, were out. They were deemed a *temptation* to young people. In my later teenage years, I was asked to do some of these things by friends from school, who were not religious. But I thought about Christ's sacrifice—and I wanted to make sure I was worth it, that Jesus did not feel He had died in vain for me.

I have given a few keynote speeches in the past, although I haven't done much since my stroke in 2005. One of my favorites is on words: how we use words, how we can devastate someone with our words, or how we can use them to bring somebody up and make a big difference. When I talk about myself, I share my personal story, going from my happy life to a tragic life to a happy life again. After all, aren't fairy tales like that? Cinderella and Snow White were happy, then sad, and they lived happily ever after.

One of my favorite speeches to give is, "What on Earth are you Doing for Heaven's Sake?" I interviewed a lot of people beforehand. I have had a lot of good responses. The premise is to understand what on earth you really want *on Earth,* that you are willing to work for, and still go to Heaven.

I also have a Thanksgiving list in my cabinet at home of all the things I am thankful for. One day, Christi came by and looked up and said, "Momma, I really like that thanksgiving list—but 'indoor plumbing,' why in the world have you got that on there?"

I said, "If you'd been where I've been, you'd be thankful every time you sat down on the inside." Sitting on a toilet is just wonderful!

She laughed, and her eyes sparkled like Daddy's did.

Later in life Christi, Jerrie Wayne, and my brother Don all had crow's feet—the beautiful laugh lines around their eyes that became deeper when they heartily laughed—just like Daddy had. Daddy had always said wrinkles were *the price you pay for living.*

I don't think the men minded, but I thought it might bother Christi. She said she didn't mind at all. They make them all look especially happy when they laugh.

I have lived a life that was paid for by the grace of others: everything from my home to my college education to my wedding. All my life, my continual prayer was that I could live in accordance with God's plan for me, so that others would never feel their money was wasted.

A few years ago, at the lectureships at Freed-Hardeman, a group of us were standing around, catching up. I was speaking to a woman directly to my right when I heard a woman ask, "Do you know Gail Barber?" Since I was already engaged in conversation, I didn't immediately stop to acknowledge her or say hello. But a friend of mine who was there with me responded to the woman, saying yes.

The woman responded to my friend saying, "Oh, our family has been keeping up with Gail for a very long time." Then she turned and left. I wanted to spend more time with her, but she was gone.

Could it be that this woman's family was the one who had paid for my education? If so, I'd like to think she already knew that her gifts and intentional prayers were not wasted.

All these years, I had done my best to be a good Christian and a kind person, and I hoped she agreed. Though it would be impossible to meet everyone who contributed to my survival and story of redemption and hope, I wish I could meet them all and say, "Thank you." *Thank you for giving me life abundant.*

My siblings and I were given a second chance, a second family, and the gift of knowing that life is not what happens to us but is instead what we make of it.

What a remarkable, glorious, flourishing gift it has been.

Chapter 35

Brothers and Sisters

"You don't choose your family.
They are God's gift to you, as you are to them."
—Desmond Tutu

As a boy and young man, Wayne always had lived with Daddy. They were lifelong companions. No matter how far the rest of us had spread apart, Wayne stayed right by his side. Like Daddy, Wayne squeezed the best out of a lemon life right into our Southern sweet tea. He'd adjusted to Frances and her children. He truly loved them and they him. He spent his life in and out of hospital care, including a two-year stay from when he was eighteen to twenty years old, in which he had the run of the hospital.

He wasn't sick. They were just trying to get him strong enough to finally amputate his legs so that he could be taught to use a prosthesis and walk by using his arms. Unfortunately, at the same time, a silent cancer was growing in his leg. Once they discovered it in 1960, they realized his hip would never be strong enough to sustain a prosthesis.

He kept to his wheelchair, doing insane tricks like propelling and balancing himself on two wheels. He could easily go down steps and with more effort, back up the steps in his wheelchair. It gave all of us anxiety, but I think Wayne liked that. He loved bringing us into the moment, knowing all of them were short.

Wayne hadn't been able to go to school. Before I went into foster care, sometimes I would come in from school and show him what I'd learned that day. During those two years he was in the hospital, the local newspaper kept up with him. He became their project. Nurses, townspeople, and staff would come by. They educated him in those two years. He left there with book knowledge.

One of his volunteer jobs during his hospital stay was to visit people who needed hope, especially those with spinal cord injuries. One man had been shot in the back and was paralyzed. The hospital staff asked Wayne to pay the man a visit. "Talk to him a little bit and he will catch on that you can be in a wheelchair and live a normal life," a nurse suggested. Wayne was always happy to visit with others.

The second Christmas he was there, the local newspaper ran a story about his progress. In the article, they asked him, "What do you want for Christmas?"

He said, "I've never had as many comic books as I would like to have." He loved comic books! Before his long hospital stay, he would just read pictures and figure out the story. And now he could read.

They made the mistake of putting his request on the front page of the local paper. Soon they had to move the beds out and clean out an *entire room* to put all the boxes of comic books that Girl Scouts, Boy Scouts, and church groups sent.

He read every one of them and then he would pass them on to the children's wards and so forth. If there was one he really liked, he would save it. From all the boxes he was sent, he ended up with a little box about twelve inches wide that he saved from all of those.

One of the nurses, a pretty girl, loved him. She loved him in every way, and they spent a lot of time together. He was a handsome man when he was young. She asked him to marry her.

He said, "It wouldn't be fair to you."

She said, "I can take care of you and your needs. I'm a nurse. I just want to be married to you."

"I'm not going to do that," he said. "I love you, but I'm not going to marry you."

He carried her picture for a long time, but he never regretted his decision.

Later, Wayne attended Heritage Christian University (formerly called International Bible College). Wayne took Bible classes and Greek, although he had never gone to elementary or high school. His comic book reading had given him a good education in the basics, and he was eager to learn.

When Jerrie and I finally had a congregation of our own, we'd hear stories of Wayne going fishing with certain members of his church. He loved his church in Nitrate City, Alabama. They were good to him and became his sponsor, so to speak. They bought him a car after he had been going there for a while. They kept his insurance paid and gave him a gas allowance each month. He visited the hospital a lot on behalf of the church and would visit shut-ins.

The preacher had a little one-room fishing shack at the lake at Steenson Hollow, which he hadn't used in a long time. After Daddy died, he let Wayne move in that little fishing cabin where he had spent a lot of his best days. He felt at home and loved being there. He met and became friends with the locals and part-time fishermen. The one-room house was perfect for him. It was furnished with only a curtain around the bathroom. It had a floor-level entry.

Wayne would get in his wheelchair and run up and down the roads. People knew him because he made friends so easily. Friends would sit with him on the lake. I wondered if he ever skipped stones across the lake's glassy surface, remembering the family we had when we were young.

A Champion performer

Wayne Champion is a familiar sight in Colbert County gathering aluminum cans from his wheelchair. Friends of Champion have helped him out with an improved form of transportation.

Wayne picking up trash, photographed for a local paper

When Jerrie and I would visit him in the summers, his swimming abilities would always impress Jerrie. “You don’t have to worry about him,” I’d say. “He can swim like a fish. He has been swimming all his life, just about.”

I loved hearing the sweet stories about my brother. The church always had a big fish fry every year. Wayne would volunteer to cut up all the onions. He said it didn’t bother him for some reason, so that was his job.

Jerrie baptized Wayne. No matter how far away Wayne was from me physically, he was a constant, just like Daddy. Not just for myself, but for Don and Brenda especially. Because they lived closer, they visited him more. They would all go fishing or shopping at "Mountain Top" outpost.

Gail, Wayne, Don, and Brenda at Christi's wedding on August 1, 1992

Don and Brenda both went to Freed-Hardeman for college. When they arrived everyone thought they were either twins or dating, since they spent so much time together and enjoyed each other's company.

After college, Don took a summer job at General Shoe Company in Centerville, Tennessee, and was a very hard worker. He worked so fast that the people working with him begged him to slow down because it made them look bad. He worked there until he returned to college and was drafted into the army. Despite Donald's strong desire to stay close to family, he was sent to Korea in 1966. As it turned out, he loved being there. He spent his spare time giving back at an orphanage that was very close to the base.

When Don was in the army, we could only write or send care packages. One Christmas, I sent a big box of homemade chocolates to him. He got it in July. He and his friends enjoyed it with spoons.

When he returned from Korea, he married a woman and decided to adopt her children. They were lucky to have found each other.

I was grateful to see Brenda and Don adopt the skills we had been taught. Both were working hard on their careers, rearing their children, and being faithful to God and the church. It fostered the belief that we were resolute, in control of our lives, and able to rise above the poverty that marked our childhood.

Don and Brenda

We Champions tried to find ways to spend some time together every year. By 1969, Jerrie and I had a house in Madisonville, Kentucky, large enough to accommodate all my family. Every Christmas and once in the summer all three of my siblings would come to our house to visit us. They would pitch in money for groceries. We would usually celebrate our Christmas get-together in January.

Don, Wayne, and Brenda would come in the front door, start telling 'Bama versus Auburn college football jokes, go straight to the kitchen table and start playing Mexican train (a dominoes game), then stay up late into the night playing games and talking. We'd have the best time. Jerrie sometimes played but was mostly at the church building working.

Don especially bonded with Jerrie over riding bikes in the cooler Tennessee summer mornings, or the strangely warm December afternoons. One summer they rode together the seventy-five miles from Centerville, Tennessee, to Linden, Tennessee, and back to his parents' house. *Somehow,* they survived. When they got back home from the actual trip, his mother was not home yet to make lunch. They were starving, so Jerrie made Don a mayonnaise sandwich. They still laugh about it being one of the nastiest things Don had ever eaten. And given our childhood, Don *knew* the worst of the worst when it came to food.

After we moved to Nashville, we would also take a day during our family visits to go to Opryland. Their facilities were very handicap friendly. Not only did they have a special entrance, but when Wayne was with us, we were put at the head of the line through a back way.

Part of my Christmas gift to my siblings was a dinner at a nicer restaurant. It was maybe 2000 when we took them to Monell's, a restaurant with homecooked Southern food on the outskirts of downtown Nashville. The next year, I had plans for another unique place, but Don asked, "Could we go back to where we went last year?" So, Monell's became tradition. It was always a wonderful treat.

We would also go bowling. For Wayne's benefit, we asked the bowling alley staff to put up the bumpers. We would play putt-putt together, too. Even in his wheelchair, Wayne did well. But mostly, we stayed home. When our children were together, they enjoyed playing with their cousins and taking naps.

As their children grew older, it became harder for me to buy them Christmas gifts since I didn't know what they wanted. I would give them money. We would go to the mall with their parents. They would buy their Christmas gift from me. The rule was they had to let me know what "I bought them."

In later years, Brenda always set the date for family visits because she was the only one of the siblings still working.

Last Champion meal at Monell's

Don was the maintenance supervisor of two large apartment complexes, a job he loved mostly because a lot of the children knew him. He would play with them in the pool. They called him Diddy. "Throw me in!" they would yell.

He began to feel unwell in 2012, so he went to the doctor, then to the hospital. Brenda was with him. She called me crying from the hallway. "Don has lung cancer," she said. After a few days, the doctors determined he had tuberculosis instead.

After several surgeries and weeks of treatment, he was able to leave the hospital. He received daily visits for months from the health department. They knew he got tuberculosis from an illegal immigrant because no legal citizen had it.

When he left the hospital, he went to Brenda's house for about six months and then was able to go back to his own apartment. His daughter, Natasha, quit her job to take care of him. It was about two years before he could go back to work. The government paid him a full salary the whole time, saying it was their fault for letting a tuberculosis patient into the country illegally. He never completely recovered.

Champions at Childhaven Reunion, June 13, 2015

After Freed-Hardeman, Brenda went to cosmetology school and trained to be a beautician. While working at the beauty shop, she met Jim, the barber next door. They dated, married, and had one son, Michael. People teased that we both married barbers.

Then, tragically, Brenda's lungs and throat started bothering her, so she quit that job in her late twenties and took a job as an assistant manager at Bruno's Grocery Store.

A Vietnam veteran, Jim suffered from Agent Orange and died when he was about forty-five years old.

One day while Wayne was driving his car, his tie rod broke, throwing him into a ditch. He broke his collarbone so he couldn't take care of himself for a while. So, after Wayne had lived in the fishing shack for a decade, Brenda invited him to move in with her. Wayne was hoping he would get to go back to thc fishing shack. He loved living in that little house by the water.

Sadly, halfway through Wayne's rehabilitation, his preacher died, and his wife told Wayne that she needed to sell the little house at Steenson Hollow Lake because she needed the money. So, Wayne continued to live with Brenda.

Brenda worked at Bruno's Grocery Store for thirty-five years as front-store manager until she retired at sixty-two. When she retired, I said, "Brenda, you've worked your entire life. You will not enjoy retirement."

I was right. She was still young, so, when a Piggly Wiggly opened near her home, she went to work for them as a clerk. She loved working there so much she stayed there until she died.

Brenda's passing was horrible. Just like almost everyone else's in my family. It was during Christmas of 2018.

Our family Christmas celebration was scheduled to be on Monday, January 21. The day before, on Sunday, she had rented a car because hers had a problem. She and Wayne were to pick it up on Monday morning and then go get Don. They were to be at our house by lunchtime.

On Sunday morning, I had already set the games out, including one new one we had never played. It was a homemade board game a man had made for me. I was so excited to teach them. The holiday visit was back to adults only.

Wayne wanted to leave his room clean, so Brenda had gotten him a broom. When he went back to the den to give it back to her, he found her unresponsive. Her iPad was still on, meaning it had been less than two minutes since she'd died. He was calling her name and shaking her when her daughter-in-law, a home health nurse, came in. She did all she could while Wayne called 911.

Paramedics did all they could on the way to the hospital, knowing it was hopeless. At the hospital, the doctors pronounced her dead. They determined an autopsy was not needed as she had died either from a massive heart attack or an aneurysm.

Call it a sign of the times. Jerrie and I found out about Brenda's death through Facebook. Jerrie and I had just gotten home from church. He was upstairs. I was in the downstairs bedroom when I heard him calling my name over and over in a very frantic voice. I thought he had fallen down the stairs.

We met in the den. He had his laptop in his hand, open to Wayne's Facebook page. Wayne had posted, "My sister, Brenda, just died."

I said, "This must be a joke. If someone hacks someone else, why would they post such an awful thing?"

It didn't occur to me that it was true. That was until we saw missed calls and messages from Don's ex-wife (they were still good friends) saying, "Please give us a call. It's important."

We later learned that Brenda had gone to church and then to work. The boss had sent her home telling her she didn't look well. At only seventy-one, Brenda was the baby of our family. The healthiest of us all. We had been sure she would see all of us buried, and now we were going to have to plan her funeral.

I called Wayne. He was inconsolable, almost hysterical.

Brenda's death is the most heartbreaking thing that has ever happened to me. I went kind of crazy. For months, I was thinking of her every minute of every day. I cried at things I would not have cried at before. I became absentminded. I stumbled, hurting myself. It was hard to concentrate. The joyous feeling in my life was gone. My brothers told me they experienced it the same way.

Naturally, Don could hardly speak about it. They were close. Inseparable. They spent their adult years living close to each other. They went to church together part of the time. They also went fishing and shopping at a place called Mountain Top where most of my Christmas presents were bought.

Brenda's only child Michael and his wife Jennifer lived with Brenda. They insisted that Wayne continue living with them.

A year after Brenda's burial, Wayne got sick. By the end of the next January, he was dead, too.

December 28, 2019, through January 10, 2020, Jerrie and I were in Israel on tour with our children and grandchildren. While there, I kept up with Facebook as I did at home. One day, Wayne posted that he was in the hospital. Every day he posted a detailed report on his Facebook page about how he was and what doctors were saying. I was anxious to get home to see him. I checked his posts every day.

Suddenly, there was nothing. No updates.

I thought, *He must have died.*

I messaged Michael who said Wayne had lost his phone. It was later found in some dirty sheets. So, Don kept us informed the best he could. When we got home, we drove to Alabama to see Wayne, but he had been placed in a medically induced coma.

When we got to the hospital, the medical staff said they could give him a shot that would wake him up for a few minutes. I told them not to put him through that, but I did go to his bed. As I stood by him, I touched him and called his name. He opened his beautiful black eyes and stared at me, and I him. I spoke to him but don't remember what I said. He never blinked. He looked like he was thinking. Then after a couple of minutes, he closed his eyes again. We went home.

Don called two days later to tell me Wayne had died. Don and I were sad but not shocked or heartbroken. When Wayne was paralyzed as a baby, doctors thought he might live to be two years old. Wayne lived to be eighty. His life expectancy only shows the determination of a Champion.

Wayne's church elders had planned a wonderful funeral for him. He was their "boy" now. Jerrie preached the funeral service, but several others spoke as well. They talked about how they and the church were so encouraged by Wayne's life. Wayne was always the first one at the door for worship services, even when all knew he wasn't well. They praised him right into Heaven.

Wayne was loved. He had a most happy life.

In my imagination, I can see Wayne and Brenda in Paradise. She is still "taking care of him." I firmly believe he is walking around all over Paradise. If there are mountains and trees to climb, he is climbing them. If there are fish in the sea, he is fishing.

I had a stroke in 2005. Then, a few days into our last trip to Israel, I felt terrible. The whole time there, I knew I was sick, and somehow I knew it was serious. I carried on the best I could but spent a lot of time sitting on the bus. Thankfully, I had been there before. I wasn't going to go home as two of our group already had (not our family). When we did get home, Jerrie took me to a hydro center. I was given two bags of fluids that helped.

I saw my doctor the next day. Knowing I was a very sick woman, he ordered a considerable number of tests. Every few days, I would get a call to come back for more tests. Finally, I said to the doctor, "I'm brave. I'm determined to do whatever I need to do. What is wrong with me?"

After a deep breath, he said, "You have chronic kidney failure." I was in shock. He then changed prescriptions that might hurt me. I had eaten something with a very bad bacteria in it. Then, he said with confidence, "At your age, you could live the rest of your life with proper care and never really have a serious problem." Christi offered me a kidney, which was incredibly sweet, but we were not a match if I needed one.

I decided I would tell no one, mainly because I didn't want to hear horror stories of someone they knew. Then one day, a good friend asked plainly, "What did the doctors tell you?" I felt like I had to get out the answer.

I said, "I have chronic kidney failure."

She said, "Oh, my mother died with that." Then, she went on to tell me her mother had been diagnosed at fifty and had died when she was eighty-three. It turned out to be a hopeful conversation.

Family Christmas 2021

Chapter 36

And Then There Was One

"O, give thanks to the Lord for His steadfast love endures forever. Grief never ends but it changes. It is a passage, not a place to stay. Grief is not a sign of weakness nor lack of faith... it is the price one pays for love."
—Psalms 107:1

"We are the Champions" no longer. "I am a Champion."

Today, on the morning of Friday, February 18, 2022, my brother, Don, died peacefully in his sleep at the age of seventy-six. His granddaughter had jumped on his bed to play and then went to tell her mother that she couldn't wake up Pappa. The paramedics said that he had died peacefully, with no trauma.

Don was a dedicated Christian man. God and his family had been Don's world these many years. He had been a greeter at his church for years. But since he had had tuberculosis, his doctor forbade him from going to church during the pandemic. Most of the membership knew him. I had prayed he would live long enough to see his precious granddaughter, Khloe, at least become a teenager.

I talked to him a few days before he died. He said, "I'm going to church tomorrow. I'll wear a double mask. I'd rather have COVID-19 than miss worship one more day." People need people. He went and never got COVID-19.

My heart is broken. All the Champions but me are dead.

Don had a most wonderful funeral. Many friends were there. The church prepared a meal for us. The week before he had forgotten to take his Bible home with him. The preacher read the scriptures from Don's own Bible. Jerrie did an excellent job, too.

I am a visual person. On Friday, I visualized a great reunion in Paradise with Don, Brenda, Wayne, Mama, and Daddy. All were so happy but so sad to see Donald there. They will have to explain to him that he is dead, as they had to tell Brenda, who had died without warning.

I believe that in Paradise, souls can still be sad and concerned about people on Earth as the "rich man" was when he asked that Lazarus in Paradise be sent to tell his five brothers not to behave badly and end up where he was in Hades in Luke 16:29-31.

At the Judgment, people will leave Paradise and Hades and go to Hell or Heaven where there will be no more tears, sadness, or sorrow (Revelations 21:4). To the thief on the cross, Jesus said, "Today, you will be with me in Paradise" (Luke 23:43). Jesus went to Heaven when he ascended from Earth (Luke 24:50).

I am extremely sad and a bit lonely knowing we will never be the Champions again until we all reunite again in Paradise or Heaven. They will be there for me, as we always took care of each other on Earth. They will show me around as I used to "show people around" at Childhaven, showing me the wonder of where we are. And I'll run into the arms of Mama and Daddy once again.

The framed portraits of Mama and Daddy are still next to my bathroom at our house. The last thing I do every night is to go to the bathroom, and as I enter, I say, "Good night" to Mama and Daddy. The portrait of the four of us children also hangs there, and I say, "Good night" to all of us too.

Remembering Steenson Hollow makes me think of my parents. I can see Mama on the shore, lovingly watching Daddy swim. And I can see a picture of his strong arms arching above the water and dipping beneath it—making waves with his big, paddling feet.

Later in life, the visions of the lake overwhelmed so many of my memories it was hard to tell which were real and which were imaginary. That's the thing about trauma—everything becomes fragmented pictures, muffled sounds, and shadowy feelings. Nothing is as you recall it. Because nothing was what it seemed. And just when your intuition is certain, you are forced to reckon with gaping holes in your memory.

These days, remembering Mama and Daddy means falling backward through time and space, connecting with a part of myself that no longer feels familiar. But one thing always will: a tranquil and perfect scene etched in my heart and mind forever.

One of the dearest memories I have left of Mama is on *the other side of the lake,* watching her drift into a summer slumber beneath my favorite tree, surrounded by Daddy and her children. Surrounded by love.

In our family, we believe God answers prayers and intervenes in our lives. I see that despite our devastation and unique experiences with death, Heaven is still brought to Earth in the midst of it. When the day is bright, and the white wisps contrast the clear blue sky, I look for my loved ones the way I did when I was a child.

Though I have long known the truth about fleecy clouds, I still find myself looking for Mama, and for Daddy, who is always beside her. And there's always one for Brenda. Wayne. And now Don. Mr. and Mrs. Mitchell. Mother Lee. Daddy Brock. James Jones. Johnny. And Del, who passed away in 2021.

God has blessed me beyond measure. I know for certain that He worked through every single person in my life—good or bad—to guide me and empower me throughout my journey. I can't help but count my blessings.

So, yes. There is a fleecy cloud for everyone—even for Mammy.

"When I remember these things, I have hope."

—Lamentations 3:21

Reflections from Gail and Jerrie's Children

Christi and Jerrie Wayne

I feel abundantly blessed that God chose me to be the daughter of my two amazing parents. Not just that, but I delight that I inherited equal parts of both.

My dad is logical, organized, methodical and almost everything is viewed through a black and white lens. My mom is carefree, creative, adventurous, and almost everything is viewed from a rainbow glitter lens. They are complete opposites, but a beautiful pairing!

I heard many of my mom's stories growing up. I clung to the fun stories, and I shielded my soul from the bad, because it was just too much to take it in. I couldn't comprehend how someone could be so cruel to a child. More than that, how could they do that to my mom?

I had an amazing childhood! My family was loved, and we loved right back. We had people in our home often. My parents planted seeds of friendship wherever they were. We had so much support and we were a part of a huge and wonderful family—the church—God's family.

My parents tried to teach us lessons in every aspect of our lives. How to share, how to be kind, how to forgive, how to be grateful.

When I was five years old, we were moving away from the only home that I knew. Madisonville, Kentucky was a wonderful place, with a loving church family. They wanted to shower us with gifts before we left. My brother and I were so lovingly embraced by so many people. I knew they would have something very special for us.

Someone left the room to retrieve our gift, and my body went from anticipation, to limp and deflated when I saw the most insulting piece of junk imaginable. My mom bent down and said, "Christi Gail, you straighten up and put a smile on your face right now!" Fighting back the tears, I whispered back, "but they gave us garbage."

The black garbage bag was set before me and Jerrie Wayne, and I squealed! It was a black bean bag, and it was amazing! It was the very best gift we had ever been given!

The bean bag went to Georgia with us and lasted all twelve years of our time there. About once a year, when it would flatten, mom would find beanbag filling around the house, such as newspaper or hay. She would fluff it up and restore it to its former glory.

Mom had that way about her with people, too. They would come to her feeling flattened. She would spend time with them, feed them, and laugh with them. Fluff them up and restore them to their former glory.

When Jerrie Wayne and I got older, we still felt the love from so many people, but we also felt our fishbowl was getting smaller. We knew that people watched the preacher's family, and that's why mom and dad tried extra hard to train us to behave in a manner that would be pleasing, but God created us to push.

We were raised in a very conservative manner, and I understand why, but when I was a teenager, I had enough of the black and white, and I needed to breath.

I was embarrassed by some of the rules. I wanted to wear shorts, I wanted to dance, I wanted to be normal.

So, I snuck shorts to school, and I snuck to school dances. That seemed harmless enough, so the rebellion continued. So much so, my parents thought James Jones could help me, too.

James became a part of our family. He understood my parents, therefore he understood me. He didn't try to piece us together like a beautiful puzzle, at first. He let us, for once, be our own puzzle, and find out our reasons why. He understood how difficult it could be to be Jerrie Barber's daughter. He understood how difficult it could be for my dad to have read all the right books, and have done all the right things, to have a child he no longer recognized, and could no longer control.

The loving people at our church also loved to tattle on me and Jerrie Wayne. I think our unruly behavior was a relief to them. Maybe their children weren't so bad after all, just look at the preacher's kids.

When a concerned mom would approach my mom with restrained delight, my mom would just smile and nod, because she knew the whole truth. She knew about that mom's child. She knew the horrible situation that caused such great concern, involved her children, too. However, my mom didn't need to tattle. That is not how she filled her cup. She knew brokenness is the only way that we can grow stronger, better, and more loving, and it is our scars that makes us beautiful.

Thankfully, my rebellious streak was short lived, and James helped us put all our pieces back together, more beautiful than before.

My mom has always been our soft place to land. She didn't need us to be perfect preacher's children. Our perfection was to allow our imperfections to shine. To grow to be adults with empathy instead of judgement. To love the less fortunate instead of being a bully. To laugh instead of complaining. To forgive instead of holding a grudge.

My mom is simply the very best, and God has been SO good to me!

—Christi Gail Parsons

Brian and Christi Parsons, Brittan and Darby Cowen, Braden Parsons

This book has been eye-opening. I always knew there was more to the story than Childhaven and Momma having a mean grandmother. Occasionally as a child, I would catch a glimpse that would quickly fade. After Wayne, Don, and Brenda would come for a visit, those glimpses were closer to the surface, but then the wall would come back up.

I have fond memories of visiting Childhaven as a child, jumping on the trampoline in the gym, staying in the cottages, and eating in the lunchroom. I can almost smell the lunchroom while writing this. I know my parents not only loved Childhaven, but there was a sense of gratefulness for them, and probably why Dad serves on their board.

Growing up with a parent who grew up in an orphanage was normal for us, just like having a father who is a minister, or living in the house that we did. It was my normal. That said, I was also aware that outside of Momma's father (PawPaw) there were many other people who were close and special, like family: the Mitchells and the Brocks. I know they were not family, but I knew I was welcome in their homes, and they were special people in our lives. Again, it was our normal.

I did not ask about the childhood of the parents of my friends. And outside of the very young childhood arguments of "my dad can beat up your dad" conversations, I did know very early on that my mother could kill chickens two at a time by ringing their necks, and she was very fast at that job. I was aware of her willingness to take risks, especially in the old swimming pool at Childhaven. I was aware that Momma had an adventurous spirit, and probably had a lot to do with why I was a bit more on the adventurous side.

Momma has a beautiful voice and sang in our home and is and was a powerful voice during worship. I believe I have inherited my love for singing from her.

I had mono when I was eight and had to spend an inordinate amount of time out of school several weeks in a row. While at home, Momma and I didn't have a lot to do other than watch old movies. What irritated me were her emotions at these old movies, always crying at the sad parts, which seemed very sappy to me. Maybe it was something that I didn't understand or maybe it was just a tender heart, but the older I get, the more I seem to identify with that side of her. Though I would never be caught shedding a tear at make-believe.

There are many things I could tell, but to sum it up, Momma was my normal. While what this book reveals may seem fantastic and extraordinary to some, it was my normal. I know that because Momma had a less than ordinary life I, and most all that know Gail, have been blessed.

—Jerrie Wayne Barber, II

Jerrie Wayne's family

Acknowledgements

In grateful appreciation to all my families:

The Champions - Daddy, Mama, Wayne, Don, Brenda.

Childhaven - Daddy Brock, Mother Lee, all the houseparents, staff, Board of Trustees, the other children who touched my life.

The Barbers - Jerrie, Jerrie Wayne, Christi.

Their Families:

Jerrie Wayne - Terri (Scott)

Elizabeth, Jeffrey Peebles - Jackson, Connor

Allie Jean

Whitney - Nathan Carroll, Zain, Asher

Dalton - Lizzie (Banks)

Wyatt Houston

Christi (Parsons), Brian

Brittan - Darby Cowan

Braden

The Family of God (my church family) - Over the first forty years, Jerrie and I worked full-time with five churches. Over the last fifteen years, Jerrie and I have worked with 10 churches as interim. Each one has blessed my life. Thank you.

My new friend and ghostwriter, Alice Sullivan.

Joey Sparks for the cover and setting the type.

The many friends, family, and strangers who read and made suggestions for improvements to my book.

A special thank you to:

Jerrie Barber

Jerrie Wayne Barber, II

Grant Dillard

Sandra & Dennis Johnson

Eddie Miller

Patti & John Miller

Christi Parsons

Anne Shelton

David Wright

Gwen Zimmerly

About the Author

Gail Champion Barber

Most of the trauma of my childhood began to be in the past, where it belonged, when I got professional help. There wasn't anyone else I trusted with all that information. My parents, especially Daddy, after Mama died, were a great encouragement to me. The staff and other children at Childhaven showed me love, encouragement, and value. But I didn't share with them my complete past. They were not prepared to help.

Secrets will display themselves in a lot of ways. They are the heaviest of burdens. Their weight gets heavier with time. Prayer, belief in God, good people—especially family, worship, and Bible study all helped.

I have found the more I tell my secrets the more people tell me theirs—many for the first time. It is a wonderful gift to me when people choose to tell me their secrets. They will be held as a sacred trust.

If you would like to communicate with me in any way, contact me:

Phone: (615)-584-7130
Email: gailchampionbarber@gmail.com

Address:

P.O. Box 210602
Nashville, Tennessee 37221

And to keep up with Gail and Jerrie's work, visit these two websites:

https://www.newshepherdsorientation.com
https://www.jerriebarber.com

Made in the USA
Columbia, SC
13 May 2025